D0812476

THE AGE OF SEGREGATION:
RACE RELATIONS IN THE SOUTH, 1890–1945

The Age of Segregation: Race Relations in the South, 1890–1945

Essays by

DERRICK BELL

MARY FRANCES BERRY

DAN CARTER

AL-TONY GILMORE

ROBERT HIGGS

GEORGE TINDALL

WITHDRAWN

Edited by
ROBERT HAWS

UNIVERSITY PRESS OF MISSISSIPPI
JACKSON 1978

Copyright © 1978 by the
University Press of Mississippi
Manufactured in the United States of America
All Rights Reserved

This volume is sponsored by the
University of Mississippi

Library of Congress Cataloging in Publication Data
Main entry under title:

The Age of segregation.

Includes bibliographical references.
  1. Southern States—Race relations—Congresses.
2. Southern States—History—1865–   Congresses.
3. Afro-Americans—Southern States—History—
Congresses.   I.   Bell, Derrick A.   II.   Haws, Robert.
F215.A38   301.45′19′6073075   78–14233
ISBN 0–87805–087–6
ISBN 0–87805–088–4 pbk.

Contents

v

Introduction

In the decade of the 1890s the southern states of the union institutionalized a system of race relations that has been described as the south's second peculiar institution. That system of race relations consigned black southerners to a status little removed from slavery. Segregation subjugated blacks, severely damaged the hopes and aspirations of whites, hampered economic development and imposed a sinister orthodoxy on the region that W. J. Cash has aptly called the "Savage Ideal." These essays from the Third Chancellor's Symposium on Southern History held at the University of Mississippi in October of 1977 concentrate on the theme of race relations during the Age of Segregation.

Derrick Bell's essay on the racial imperative in American law provides a general introduction to the problem of segregation. As C. Vann Woodward has written, "law has a special importance in the history of segregation, more importance than some sociologists would allow, and . . . the emphasis on legal history is justified." [1] Professor Bell personifies that rather rare combination of scholar and activist. He is a distinguished scholar,[2] and

---

1. C. Vann Woodward, *The Strange Career of Jim Crow*, 2nd Revised Edition, New York: Oxford University Press, 1966, ix.

2. *Race, Racism and American Law*, Boston: Little, Brown, 1973.

the first black faculty member of the Harvard Law School. In the 1960s he spent enough time in Mississippi as a civil rights attorney that he paid Mississippi state income taxes.

Dr. Mary Frances Berry discusses the more informal dimension of racial discrimination in her essay. Trained in both history and law at the University of Michigan, she was a well-known historian and university administrator before becoming Assistant Secretary for Education in the Department of Health, Education and Welfare in the spring of 1977.[3]

The system of segregation had a great impact on white southerners as well as black southerners. This impact on whites and its influence on southern politics in the first half of the twentieth century are discussed by Dan Carter, Mellon Professor of the Humanities at Emory University. Professor Carter is the author of a prize-winning study of the Scottsboro Boys and his work is invariably characterized by a mastery of the subject and crackling prose.[4]

Blacks responded to the agony of segregation in a variety of ways that ranged from almost complete acquiescence through tempered resistance to outright revolt. Professor Al-Tony Gilmore, Director of the Afro-American Studies Program at the University of Maryland, outlines this pattern. For documentation his essay relies on a careful blend of folktales and systematic protest writing. He is, likewise, well-qualified, having written a fascinating account of the career of Jack Johnson, the great black heavyweight boxing champion.[5]

For some time, economists have pointed out the detrimental economic consequences of racial discrimination. Systematic dis-

---

3. *Military Necessity and Civil Rights Policy: Black Citizenship and the Constitution, 1861–1868*, Port Washington, N.Y.: Kennikat, 1977.

4. *Scottsboro: A Tragedy of the American South*, Baton Rouge: Louisiana State University Press, 1969.

5. *Bad Nigger! The National Impact of Jack Johnson*, Port Washington, N.Y.: Kennikat, 1975.

crimination denied blacks a legitimate return from their labor, and consequently deepened southern poverty. This development is refined by Robert Higgs, a professor of economics at the University of Washington. Professor Higgs' research into the economics of discrimination has established him as one of the leading authorities in the field.[6]

This book of essays concludes with an assessment of the costs of segregation by George B. Tindall, Kenan Professor of History at the University of North Carolina, Chapel Hill. Professor Tindall is the outstanding historian of the twentieth century South and the author of a number of distinguished works on southern history.[7] He points out we do not yet have sufficient perspective to accurately calculate the cost of the segregation to the South and the nation. However, the story contained in these essays bares ample testimony to the fate that awaits the South and the nation should the drive toward racial equality ever be abandoned.

In editing these essays for the department of history, I would like to thank Chancellor Porter L. Fortune, Jr., for the support provided by the University of Mississippi and Professors H. Dale Abadie, Frederick E. Laurenzo, David G. Sansing and Michael V. Namorato for support provided by the department of history.

Robert J. Haws
University, Mississippi

---

6. *Coercion and Competition: Blacks in the American Economy, 1865–1914,* New York: Cambridge University Press, 1977.

7. *The Emergence of the New South, 1913–1945,* Baton Rouge: Louisiana State University Press, 1967.

THE AGE OF SEGREGATION:
RACE RELATIONS IN THE SOUTH, 1890–1945

The Racial Imperative in American Law

DERRICK A. BELL, JR.

Introduction

Rayford W. Logan portrayed America's post–Reconstruction years for black people as the "Nadir."[1] The description is not extravagant. It defines well the depths to which blacks were reduced, and the nature of the betrayal which brought the freedmen low. The law's involvement in that downfall and its consequences could not have been greater. One wonders, had the country fallen into anarchy during the half-century from 1890 until World War II, whether disregard for the rights, property, and the very humanity of blacks would have been greater than, in fact, it was during that bleak time.

The speculation need not be prolonged. For all black people some of the time, and for most southern blacks all the time, it was worse than anarchy. It was war. The South, having failed to overcome the North's superior manpower and armaments, resorted to force again, this time against the unarmed blacks in their midst. The North, having freed the slaves, expressed initial concern, then lost interest in the freedmen. Somehow, it no longer seemed worth their involvement. One-sided wars, like one-sided sports events, seldom hold the attention of spectators for very long.[2]

And what of the law? The courts, as the Vietnam experience

most recently illustrates, are not eager to adjudicate the legality of armed conflict, whether or not officially declared.[3] Post-Reconstruction courts were not different. Judges were content to take sides by doing nothing. They exerted only that energy required to so narrowly construe seemingly applicable constitutional provisions and civil rights statutes, that one ponders why the Congress had labored at such length to produce laws that impressed the judiciary so little.

Serious consideration of post-Reconstruction America remains a more painful than rewarding enterprise for even the more scholarly of the descendants of those veterans who managed to survive a conflict that was no less deadly because unacknowledged. Indeed, if the period were now no more than a nightmare fading fast in the light of a newer, more equality-oriented day, there would be little occasion for the attention we shall direct here to that bitter, bloody time. Even the significance distillable from our presence in this southern setting, itself an important site in later racial battles, barely warrants dredging up so much history that strains, even today, those bonds of shared humanity upon which a lasting society across lines of race and color must be built.

But the events and particularly the legal developments of those years contain great contemporary significance, and may prove of crucial concern to all who labor to conform the country's legal performance with the Constitution's commands. A constitution that would include protection for, as well as recognition of, black rights has long been the goal. But from the nation's beginning there has been in its law, as in its behavior, an accepted incongruity on the sensitive subject of racial equality. Created for the express purpose of recognizing and protecting individual rights, America has regularly ignored the rights of blacks whenever the oversight aided economic and political interests deemed more important.

The repetitive nature of a national policy that, when faced

with a choice, so regularly sets white interests over black rights, defies a purely fortuitous explanation. One seeks rather some unspoken but universally heard and acknowledged command that condemns the country's largest minority—or most of it—to a cyclical progression with brief intervals of advance and hope followed by inevitable crisis and decline. An examination of the law's reaction to these systematic signals during the period from 1890 to World War II may enable us to identify and at least outline the motivations in American law for what might fairly be called this Racial Imperative.

A Two-Hundred-Year Prelude to Reconstruction

Precedent as well as, perhaps, the necessity for subsequent world policy was formulated in those early seventeenth-century Virginia colonies. Feeling their way toward democratic government, they determined to confound both logic and morality by enslaving blacks.[4] Today, historians generally accept the theory that economic and political advantage explain the colonial acquiescence in slavery, a decision that quickly imported to the new world the very worst practices of the old. But surely, it took more than Eli Whitney's cotton gin and an insatiable lust for power and profit to maintain an inhuman system that everyone feared, and from which relatively few became rich.[5]

More importantly for this inquiry, why did the courts so readily acquiesce in and contribute to the intricate network of slave codes that provided legal legitimacy to what in this country should have been an abhorrent concept.

By the time the Declaration of Independence proclaimed a rebellion to obtain and protect "unalienable rights of life, liberty and the pursuit of happiness," the paradox of fashioning and enforcing slave laws had become an accepted habit. When the American Revolution proved successful, slavery was too settled to consider abolition seriously. The exceptions were in those areas where slaves were few and the opposition to blacks, slave or free, was correspondingly great. Abolitionists focused their attacks on slavery's moral evils and its inappropriateness in a country dedicated to the principle of human equality, but the major push for emancipation actions in the North stemmed from other factors. Businessmen who could not efficiently use slaves, and laborers who did not wish to compete with slaves for jobs, opposed the institution. Both groups hoped emancipation would lessen fears of slave revolts and decrease generally the number of blacks in their midst.[6] Even so, it must have required more than a simple desire to maintain an established, economically important institution or a firm belief in the superiority of the white race, to both sanction and shield slavery in a constitution whose preamble mandates "Liberty to ourselves and our Posterity." Did the founding fathers, representing North and South, have no greater motivation than their determination to keep the fledgling country together when they agreed to compromises on the issue of slavery?

When, seventy-five years later, three new constitutional amendments abolished slavery and gave blacks *de jure* entitlement to citizenship,[7] it appeared that the chains that linked whites to racist solutions for every domestic ill also had been broken. The appearances were a mirage. Industrial capitalism in particular, and the white working class in general, sought an end to the threat that slavery posed.[8] Freeing blacks was a necessary but, for many, an unfortunate concomitant of abolition. Given that fact, the failure of Reconstruction was foreordained.

Spurred by prospects of economic and political benefit to both, the North and South made peace, cementing their mutual interests in another compromise, the catalyst for which was the surrender without ceremony of the former slaves to their former masters.[9] Black people and their hopes had again fallen victim to the Racial Imperative. The devastation they suffered as a result was worse because it struck now at a people whose liberty was measured in the main by the loss of that dominion-based protection slaveowners extended to their human property.[10] Even this dubious guardianship, when compared with federal and state efforts to safeguard the lives and well-being of the freedmen, had provided more security than anything the law was able to offer for half a century.

Post-Reconstruction Law in National Context

During blacks' far from gentle slide back toward a condition which, measured purely in terms of physical protection, was as bad as slavery, why were courts so unable to safeguard and, generally, so uninterested in black rights? An explanation requires placing post-Reconstruction courts in the context of their more general functioning at that time. In the final decades of the nineteenth century, American courts had become first the espousers and then the creators and propagators of a conservative ideology that permeated all aspects of American life. Called upon to decide pressing questions concerning the relations of labor and capital, the power of state legislatures, and the rights of big business, the courts foreswore impartiality and came down heavily on the side of economic interests. The shift from a stand of noninterference in questions of economic and legislative policy mirrored other changes that were occurring in American society during this era.[11]

In the 1880s, American society was rife with social tensions. There were cries from the society's lower-income echelons for free silver, labor rights, a graduated income tax, and protection against the trusts.[12] These demands were countered by an ideology which embraced the established order of things and the immutability of prevailing social patterns. Charles Darwin, Herbert Spencer, William Graham Sumner, and other influential social scientists combined to champion a system that supported natural rights and racial purity and that equated wealth and power with virtue.[13] Immigrants in the North and blacks in the South were seen as corrupting forces, entities to be discounted in the formulation of public policy. Popular democracy and, with it, universal suffrage became suspect, and a return to property and literacy qualification was urged.[14]

The Supreme Court, sympathetic to conservative interests through the pattern of its past decisions, its duties as preserver of the law, and its specific composition at the time, became in these decades the major protector of propertied interests.[15] Courts formulated due process and freedom of contract doctrine to shield business from state regulation, denied rights to labor, outlawed the federal income tax, and watered down the Sherman Anti-Trust laws.[16] Having recast its image and reputation after the debacle of *Dred Scott,* the Court expanded its role from interpreter to a principal maker of law, and became the central paradox in a paradoxical age of conservative reform. It espoused individual rights at the expense of the individual and acted in behalf of public interest through the protection of private enterprise.

Within this framework, racial law became an important conduit for the preservation and legitimation of the established order. Shaken by fears of a powerful coalition of white Populists and blacks, white conservatives in the South turned to disfranchisement as well as legal separation in social and economic spheres. Race distinction, an instrument of popular suppression in other eras of American history, was once more brought forth by an elite wishing to maintain power. Here, too, the courts were the espousers of conservative sentiment. Though eager to countermand state regulation in the economic realm, the justices were satisfied to leave state regulation of race relations untrammeled during these years. The Court first reduced privileges and immunities under federal protection. Later, it invalidated the public accommodation provisions of the 1875 Civil Rights Act, and finally formulated the separate but equal doctrine that sustained segregation for three generations.[17] Court policy thus followed the swing toward conservatism evidenced in the political and economic realms. The courts and along with them the rule of law became not impartial arbiters of societal relations but instead the mirror and enforcer of property interests.

Racially Discriminatory Law in the Post-Reconstruction Era
To illustrate how this judicial philosophy was brought to bear in racial cases, one need but review four key areas where needed legal protection was withheld—physical violence, disfranchisement, economic exploitation, and segregation laws. But, as will be seen, the inability of blacks to gain recognition of even their most basic rights in the post-Reconstruction era was neither a capricious act of history nor the simple manifestation of a conservative court. It resulted neither from a too-ready acceptance of scientific views of the time that boasted Caucasian superiority over all other racial groups, nor from any idealistic sense that if left to the tender mercies of southern political and economic forces, blacks would finally—through such sponsorship—gain the citizenship rights promised by the post–Civil War amendments. There was something more than even the combined force of all these motives can explain. The Racial Imperative was at work everywhere, influencing decisions, and supplying rationales for further black suppression that defied logic but somehow satisfied—for a time—needs that it alone could create. A search for it, even a futile search, should at least prove instructive.

VIOLENCE AND THE LAW. Even had the courts been philosophically inclined or morally motivated, they would have faced the greatest difficulty stemming the tide of antiblack violence, race riots, and lynchings which during the post–Civil War and post–Reconstruction periods swept in massive waves across the South, and much of the North. The atrocities were, of course, not discouraged by periodic reassurance that the courts and law enforcement agencies would make no serious effort to protect blacks by prosecuting whites.[18]

The courts early had limited their potential effectiveness by strictly construing the Reconstruction amendments. The Four-teenth Amendment, for example, was interpreted as applying only to the official acts of state officials, not to the private acts of individuals who were the main perpetrators of antiblack vio-lence.[19] Even outrages such as the 1872 Colfax Massacre in Louisiana did not shake the Court's determination to remain aloof from what became, in part by its abstention, a legally con-doned bloodbath.[20]

The Justice Department had indicted ninety-six people and succeeded in convicting nine of them in the Colfax incident, which started with an election dispute. On the governor's orders, a building that was to be used as a courthouse was seized by a posse of blacks. Excited by rumors that blacks were about to at-tack, whites burned the building and shot the blacks as they came out. Convictions were obtained, not for murder, but for conspiracy to prevent blacks from exercising rights protected by the Constitution and the Civil Rights Acts. The Supreme Court in *United States* v. *Cruikshank* reversed as to each count of the in-dictment.[21]

The Court in the *Cruikshank* case, as in other cases during the period, repeatedly read the Fourteenth Amendment as imposing on the federal government the obligation to ensure that the states did not interfere with constitutional rights, but holding the states and not the federal government with the duty to intercede when one individual interfered with the constitutional rights of others.[22] Such rulings posed little protection against the lynch murders of blacks that reached their peak in the 1890s when official reports listed almost two hundred victims of lynching each year. In the first decade of the twentieth century, the number of lynchings dropped to about one hundred per year, but the percentage of victims who were black increased.[23]

Moreover, the pattern of violence persisted as the century wore on. The Ku Klux Klan, outlawed in 1869, reorganized in

Georgia in 1915 and reached a peak membership thought to be five million in the mid-twenties. Immediately following World War I, racial violence increased. There were twenty-five race riots in the latter half of 1919.[24] In reaction to the postwar race riots, a number of states legislated against the activities of the Ku Klux Klan, prohibiting the wearing of masks or hoods in public places, night-riding, and other forms of intimidation. By 1950, nineteen states had enacted such statutes. As early as 1919, the NAACP began to work toward the passage of a federal law against lynching. In 1921, a bill was introduced on the floor of the House and passed 230 to 119, despite the opposition of southern congressmen. However, a southern-led Senate filibuster prevented a vote on the measure, and eventually the Senate voted to abandon the bill. Other similar bills, such as the Costigan-Wagner bill of 1935 and Wagner Gavagan bill of 1940, were introduced, but none was passed.[25]

Much of the violence, far from mindless, was intended to intimidate blacks who voted or otherwise attempted to become involved in politics. The withdrawal of federal troops from the 1878 elections served as the silent but universally heard signal that electoral contests could more advantageously be waged by bullet than ballot. For those who didn't get the message, it was rebroadcast through the white supremacy campaigns of the 1890s. Evidently, no tale of black atrocity was too bizarre to be given quick credence by the white mind, particularly when elections were near. The retaliatory power mounted by whites in response to rumor was so great as to give the most courageous blacks pause before taking action that would provide white mobs with actual facts. After the election of 1898 in Wilmington, North Carolina, a mob of four hundred white men set a black newspaper office on fire and killed eleven blacks.[26] But violence and intimidation were practiced prior to, as well as in the wake of, elections that paved the way toward disfranchisement. A Republican campaigning to be a convention delegate in Mississippi in 1890 was shot. Opposition to the Democrats virtually disappeared thereafter.[27]

DISFRANCHISEMENT. Historians for some years have engaged in vigorous debate as to whether the flood of black disfranchisement provisions placed in state statutes and constitutions during the decades after 1890 served as a *fait accompli* for work already accomplished by violence and intimidation, or whether affirmative legal steps were necessary to supplement the courts' silent acquiescence in stripping from blacks rights granted in the Fourteenth and Fifteenth Amendments.[28] The *fait accompli* theory would seem the more credible approach, particularly in that the legal procedures were themselves accomplished through fraud, bribery, intimidation, and violence.[29] In any event, once the disfranchisement movement began rolling between 1888 and 1893,[30] there is little record that it was greatly slowed by counterattacks of conscience.

Constitutional conventions and their subsequent deliberations followed a predictable pattern in the five states where they were called—Mississippi, South Carolina, Louisiana, Alabama, and Virginia.[31] An initial step required overcoming opposition from dissenting political groups, and the exclusion of blacks from the vote by violence, fraud, or hastily enacted voting restrictions.[32] Having garnered the votes for the calling of a constitutional convention and the election of sympathetic delegates, the conventions proceeded, not as forums for state debate on the pressing problems of the day, but as gatherings of state Democrats eager to solve only one problem—the removal of blacks as a factor in state politics.[33] After these conventions altered the state constitutions to include suffrage restrictions that were neutral as to race but had the effect of barring all blacks and many poor whites as well, the new constitutions were frequently simply proclaimed.[34]

The Democrats feared a popular vote might defeat the constitutional changes.

Other southern states adopted disfranchisement provisions without calling a constitutional convention. Between 1900 and 1908, North Carolina, Texas, and Georgia amended the suffrage clauses of their state constitutions through referenda. Florida, Tennessee, and Arkansas, with a combination of the poll tax and registration, multiple-box or secret ballot rules achieved disfranchisement by state legislative action.[35]

Through these legislative proceedings a plethora of restrictive measures were handed down. As J. M. Kousser has noted, "Each state became a laboratory for testing one device or another."[36] A number of simple voting restrictions were instituted prior to the passage of more complicated, constitutional provisions. Such basic restrictions as the registration rules, which proliferated in numerous varieties, the multiple-box law, and the secret ballot were quite effective in their own right in reducing the popular vote. Registration laws discouraged voting in a number of ways. Either the time or place of voting could be deliberately made inconvenient for registrants. For example, after 1892, Alabama held registration only in May when farmers were the busiest in the field. Registration deadlines were often set months before an election when voters were not interested or aware of campaign issues. Specific information about birth, residency, age, and occupation could be required. These requirements also worked against blacks who, as former slaves, frequently did not know their exact ages and who lived in areas that often lacked house numbers. Sometimes it was required to bring a registration certificate to the polls. Often the appointees of the state, the puppets of local Democrats, or the subjects of their own political or personal prejudices, the registrars, who had wide discretion in deciding who fulfilled registration requirements, injected further discrimination into the application of the laws. Residency requirements, too, took their toll, usually requiring a tenure of one or two years in the state and some amount of time in the county. These laws disadvantaged farm laborers who frequently moved. The multiple-box laws and the secret ballot put the illiterate at a disadvantage. The multiple-box law required voters to place their ballots in the appropriate box, usually a box being provided for each type of office up for election or for the separation of national and state elections. The secret ballot, heralded as a mechanism of reform in North and South, was also a kind of literacy requirement, substituting an often confusing public ticket for ballots which had been handed out by individual political parties privately to voters. Since in seven out of the eleven southern states, the majority of blacks could be classified as illiterate in 1900, the impact of even an indirect literacy requirement was severe.[37]

Florida, Tennessee, and Arkansas added only the poll tax to these basic provisions in order to effectuate disfranchisement. In many of the other southern states these measures were preliminaries used to mute the opposition vote in the effort to push through more extensive constitutional disfranchisement measures. The poll tax was employed in all the former Confederate states by 1904. Another, less significant provision was that of disqualification for certain crimes, the list varying from state to state but generally including such acts as bribery, burglary, theft, and obtaining money or goods under false pretenses. Literacy tests, property tests, understanding and character clauses, and the grandfather clause generally completed the disfranchisement arsenal. Still later, as blacks became better educated, more economically secure, and hence more likely to meet the suffrage qualifications, white primaries became popular, restricting the Democratic and only significant primary in those one-party states to white voters.[38]

An intricate weave of sectional and national pressures directed the South toward its disfranchisement programs. Republicans and Populists began to lose strength as the result of the defeat of the Lodge Elections Bill, the death of several key Republican leaders, the shift of the nation's attention to economic problems, and the creation of a stable national Republican majority that no longer needed the South to control the federal government.[39] Without opposition, Democrats were able to pursue suffrage restrictions which they deemed necessary in order to legalize the exclusion of black voters in case voting Republicans, back in power at the national level, might attempt to restore the black vote.

The disfranchising forces chose to act, not only due to a weakening of the opposition, but because they wished to strengthen their own position. White Democrats believed that the elimination of blacks, and some poor whites as well, from the polls would insure Democratic domination of state politics. Fearing, sometimes correctly, that blacks held the balance of power in many elections, they sought to deter blacks from supporting Republicans or other opposing groups.[40] Rather than continuing efforts to win black votes, which generally required intimidation or fraud, Democrats in most southern states concluded it made more sense to simply prevent blacks, and sometimes some white opposition forces, from voting at all. Moreover, the Democrats were concerned that continued corruption in elections would lead to the inevitable contesting of elections by opposition groups, the possible renewal of federal intervention, and even internal political disintegration if the deceptions became too severe. Paradoxically, disfranchisement of blacks became the key to the elimination of fraud and corruption by whites in the election process.[41] With blacks out of the electorate, there would no longer be the need for fraud. Repeatedly, the adoption of voting restrictions displayed what one commentator, Charles Mangum, termed "the strange picture of one race disfranchising another to save itself from the consequences of its own vices."[42] In addition, efficient government was furthered by disfranchisement, because with this "final solution" to the voting controversy, states could move on to consideration of other important problems.[43] Many of these problems were not race-connected. But as has happened again and again throughout history, adherence by the socioeconomically privileged, in this case the white Democrats,[44] to the Racial Imperative enabled them to protect and further their interests against competing whites as well as blacks.

The crusade of Democratic southerners for suffrage restriction also harmonized with changes in the national political philosophy. In the late nineteenth century, mass suffrage became suspect and a move for a literate and propertied electorate was begun. Suffrage restriction was aimed toward immigrants as well as blacks. Thus the voices of Democrats calling for "white supremacy" were joined by the more genteel intonations of upper-class reformers who embraced Darwin's notion of survival of the fittest and a return to a Federalist philosophy which championed the propertied classes. Imperialism abroad was also consonant with these elitist leanings and buttressed the arguments of those withholding rights from minorities at home.[45]

Litigation protesting the disfranchisement provisions and the white primaries was filed in state and federal courts. The decisions, in the main, upheld the rights of states to fashion their own suffrage provisions. Often ruling on technical grounds or declaring the Reconstruction amendments and legislation inapplicable to state legislation, most disfranchisement devices were allowed to stand.

In *Giles* v. *Harris*,[46] a typical case, the plaintiff charged that the disfranchising clauses of the Alabama Constitution were designed to prevent blacks from voting and thus violated the Fourteenth and Fifteenth Amendments. The Supreme Court responded first with sophistry, indicating that a court of equity cannot enforce registration under statutory provisions which the plaintiff himself is contending are invalid. The Court added that a court of equity could not enforce political rights, and on this technical ground denied the request for an injunction requiring the state to permit six thousand blacks to vote. Plaintiffs had alleged "that the great mass of the white population intends to keep the blacks from voting." If that were the case, Justice Holmes, speaking for the Court, responded, it would do little good to give black voters an order that would be ignored at the local level. Then virtually concluding the Court's impotency in political cases, Holmes added, "Apart from damages to the individual, relief from a great political wrong if done, as alleged, by the people of a state and the state itself, must be given by them or by the legislative and political department of the Government of the United States."[47] The Supreme Court did finally outlaw the grandfather clause, ruling that the provision in Oklahoma's constitution was in direct violation of the Fifteenth Amendment.[48] Later the white primary fell before a succession of legal assaults, but the most important victories came after World War II, and it was to be two decades more before potentially effective voting rights legislation would be enacted. By that time the courts had acquiesced for almost a century in all but the most blatant disfranchisement schemes.[49]

ECONOMIC EXPLOITATION. Disfranchisement of blacks meant more to whites than white superiority at the polls; it also closed off possible political remedies for the widespread economic exploitation that reduced many blacks to the status of slaves without chains. Industry, voluntarily and by statute,[50] excluded blacks from the better jobs, and segregated them into the work that was hot, hard, dirty, and dangerous.[51]

Black workers were overworked and underpaid, but if they received any wage at all, they were likely the envy of the thousands of black tenant farmers and sharecroppers whose contracts were supported by a series of statutes designed to enable white landowners to exercise almost total dominion over black lessees. If slavery had required written contracts, it is hard to imagine how such documents, in practical effect, could have been more harsh than the agreements under which blacks in the post-Reconstruction period labored, often only to find themselves sinking deeper into debt.[52]

Many state statutes provided for the criminal punishment of laborers held to have defaulted on their civil contracts without the consent of the employer, before the expiration of the contract, or who made a contract with a third party without giving notice of the prior contract. Statutes authorized arrest and jail for a whole array of activities associated with unemployment: loitering, drifting, vagrancy, disorderly conduct, etc.[53] Other statutes enabled whites to pay the fines of those convicted on a contract, requiring the freed individual to work for the surety until the value of the fine was paid.[54] If the individual defaulted before the debt was paid, a much heavier penalty could be imposed. Taken together, these statutes concerning laborers and tenants were instrumental in maintaining the large population of black tenant farmers and sharecroppers in virtual servitude during the latter nineteenth and early twentieth centuries.

The courts had early recognized the worst of these statutes for what they were, the coerced payment of labor, by means of criminal proceedings, of a purely civil liability arising from breach of contract.[55] The Supreme Court had acknowledged in the *Slaughterhouse Cases*[56] that peonage was proscribed by the Thirteenth Amendment, but was slow in applying this conclusion to the many laws and practices used to accomplish this purpose.

Not until after they had been in effect for several decades did the courts begin to strike down those statutes creating a virtual state of peonage or involuntary servitude clearly prohibited under the Thirteenth Amendment and civil rights statutes. Innovative legislators replaced the voided laws with new measures intended to maintain landlord control over tenant farmers. One version made it a criminal offense to enter into a

contract with intent to defraud. Any failure or refusal to perform
the work called for in the contract was *prima facie* evidence of
fraudulent intent, punishable as a criminal offense. Some state
courts approved such provisions,[57] and a long court battle was
required before the Supreme Court held such rules unconstitutional in *Bailey* v. *Alabama*.[58] In its decision, the Supreme Court
gave substantial weight to the fact that the Alabama law was
enforced using a local evidential rule that denied an accused
person the right to testify for the purpose of rebuffing the statutory presumption with respect to his "uncommunicated motives,
purpose, or intention."[59]

Other states, having no such rule of evidence, used this fact
as the grounds on which to distinguish and hence retain otherwise similar statutes.[60] In fact, as late as 1944, the Court was
able to rely on the *Bailey* precedent in striking Georgia and
Florida statutes that were not materially different.[61]

SEGREGATION LAWS   The imposition of laws requiring the racial
separation of blacks and whites in every conceivable activity,
like an enameled finish on a well-crafted piece of furniture,
served to highlight and symbolize a structure that was constructed through violence, disfranchisement, and economic exploitation. As in the basic construction, the law's role in the
segregation process was large and crucial.

The *Civil Rights Cases* of 1883[62] paved the way for many
of the Jim Crow laws. Coming on the heels of a number of
other decisions limiting the scope of the Fourteenth and
Fifteenth Amendments and the Civil Rights Acts, the Supreme
Court held the Civil Rights Act of March 1, 1875, unconstitutional. The act had provided for equal access to inns, public
conveyances and places of public amusement. In *Hall* v. *de
Cuir*,[63] the Supreme Court earlier had ruled in 1877 that a state
could not prohibit segregation on a common carrier. Later, the
Court's 1896 *Plessy* v. *Ferguson*[64] decision concluded separate

coach laws were not in conflict with the equal protection laws of the Fourteenth Amendment as long as equality of accommodations existed.

State statutes requiring the segregation of railroad cars had been enacted as early as 1881 when a Tennessee law was passed, according to its preamble, to protect blacks from being charged first-class fares and then forced to ride in second-class cars where smoking was allowed and obscene language was frequently used.[65] Most states, for varying reasons, had passed similar laws prior to the *Plessy* "separate but equal" decision.[66] During the next several years, there was a wave of Jim Crow laws and ordinances passed covering electric and street cars. The trend spread to boats, steamships, waiting rooms, restaurants, hotels, restrooms, water fountains, and motor carriers.[67] Segregation was also practiced in various states in hospitals and other public institutions, amusements, and residential areas.[68]

The separation by race having been deemed a reasonable regulation well within the state's police powers, the Supreme Court evidenced less concern for the "equality" portion of the *Plessy* equation. Public schools and private colleges could be segregated, and if conditions required the closing of a county's only black high school, it was, even for Justice Harlan, the great dissenter in The *Civil Rights Cases* and *Plessy* v. *Ferguson*, ridiculous for the plaintiffs to require that the white high school be closed simply to comply with the "separate but equal" doctrine.[69]

DISCRIMINATION OF THE COURTS.   The thrust of this discussion of violence, disfranchisement, economic exploitation, and segregation laws does not, regrettably, exhaust the arsenal utilized by those who fought and won the counter–Civil War. The law condoned and often undergirded each of these four weapons. But there was here, as in most wars, a fifth column, an unmentioned but vital component in the massive effort to relieve the newly freed blacks of all meaningful aspects of their emancipation. The fifth column was, of course, the courts themselves.

The courts worsened the already precarious position of those blacks who came before them, both by their decisions and through their internal practices and procedures. Whether as plaintiffs seeking justice in the courts, or as defendants facing criminal charges, blacks met with formal and informal lines of discrimination. There were few black judges or lawyers, and by custom, blacks were often barred from serving as jurors or witnesses. Even assuming the presence in some courts of nonbiased judges and effective lawyers, black defendants' chances of avoiding conviction were slim because so much of the law was written to discriminate against them.[70]

This was particularly true when the criminal charges involved interracial sex or marriage, both of which were prohibited in every southern state and many states outside the South as well. These statutes, and the vigor with which they were enforced, seemed to reflect white fears that reached the level of obsession. Whites seemed to assume that blacks, having been exploited economically and politically, would—if given the chance—retaliate not with armed attacks on white men, but with invincible sexual advances on white women. An army of psychologists have since attempted to explain this irrational conviction. Most courts, without awaiting any explanation, simply accepted the reasoning of the legislatures and approved the validity of antimiscegenation laws.[71] The Supreme Court approved Alabama's law in 1883;[72] and so powerful was the interracial-sex mythology involved in these statutes, that they were not declared unconstitutional until 1964.[73]

Every facet of court procedure became a basis for racial discrimination. Adequate counsel was seldom available to black defendants. Exclusion of blacks from inevitably all-white and, often, highly prejudiced juries, was more the rule than the exception.[74] Intimidation of potential witnesses, the disappearance of evidence, prejudicial jury charges, shockingly high sentences, even the threat, not infrequently carried out, of mob violence in case the trial did not lead—and swiftly—to the community's view of appropriate justice, were all familiar themes in reports of southern trials, particularly in cases where black defendants were charged with transgressing one of the myriad of racial mores.[75]

As early as 1880, the Supreme Court had voided statutes and court policies that systematically excluded all blacks from jury service, but the opinions made clear that Negro defendants were not entitled to a jury containing members of their race.[76] Acting on this suggestion, prosecutors were able easily to avoid systematic exclusion, while managing to maintain all-white juries in those jurisdictions where any effort was made to comply with Supreme Court rules.

Thus while *causes célèbres* such as the *Scottsboro* cases[77] might be reversed by the Supreme Court, these infrequent cases did not break the momentum of a law enforcement system which saw as its principal task the maintenance of a people legally free in a status that resembled as closely as possible the slavery supposedly banned by the Thirteenth Amendment.

Considering the available evidence in the areas surveyed and many others not here mentioned, there should be more than enough clues at this point to identify the elusive Racial Imperative that provoked such paranoid behavior by southerners for a half-century after the most important issue of Reconstruction was resolved in their favor. An answer lurks in the manic excessiveness with which restrictions in each area were designed and enforced. Actions were taken swiftly and without regard to consequences. There was intent, and the intent was invidious, but it also had a driven, reckless quality more appropriate in the unarmed pursued than in the heavily armed pursuers. Following World War I, when one would have expected the nation, flush with success in saving the world from oppression, to view its long oppressed blacks with new humanity, the opposite occurred.

Blacks were killed by the score and their property burned in riots across the North and South.

Before reaching conclusions as to the imperative capable of stirring so much racial passion, a view from the vantage point provided by our late-twentieth-century position should add a valuable perspective, for as we shall see, the view of the present reveals a striking resemblance to the just discussed past.

The Imperative's Contemporary Effects

In our time, two decades of hard-won racial reform that seemed permanent are now threatened. Those whites whose decisions set policy in this country seem again to be opting for directions which, like those in 1890, promise irrationally but—evidently—irresistibly domestic salvation in exchange for a diminishing of civil rights concerns. The courts, after a period of only partially effective resistance, apparently are moving in step with a trend to which eventual capitulation has become the familiar and predictable result. Comparisons in the past with current conditions are all too easy to discern.

The reliance on raw violence and naked terror of the post-Reconstruction years has been replaced by tactics that are more subtle but, arguably, little less efficient. Disadvantage, the heritage of past, overt discrimination stretching back to slavery, today bars most blacks from meaningful employment, effective education, and the other prerequisites for full participation in this society.[78] Jim Crow policies are obsolete because they are not needed to bar blacks from facilities that only the employed can afford. And those blacks who manage to enter the better jobs, schools, or neighborhoods, serve, often unintentionally, as manipulable proof both that the society is open and that advancement is available to those interested enough to work for it. Such an opportunity is not of value to people whose motivation has been deadened by defeat. Self-help programs are not remedies for this condition, but simply prescriptions for further failure.

Current judicial disenchantment with racial issues is characterized by the setting of standards for proving discrimination that are almost impossible to meet.[79] These standards would have been no barrier to post-Reconstruction statutes with their often blatantly discriminatory provisions. But today's challenges are to racially neutral policies. They are not irrational in their content, but in their effect have a disproportionately adverse impact on blacks and other minorities. Job seniority rules that were initiated at a time when only whites were hired are one example of such restrictive measures. Zoning rules prohibiting the construction of housing for low-income families are another. Neighborhood school assignment policies are a third, and resort to such election procedures as "at-large" voting to dilute black voter strength can be a fourth.[80]

The net result of increasing judicial approval of these restrictive measures, many of which are motivated by discriminatory intent, is to reduce the courts' responsibility for protecting rights and opportunities that are as effectively withdrawn by these techniques as anything the post-Reconstruction period could offer. Their effectiveness can be measured by the large and growing disparity in black-white income and unemployment statistics, the growing isolation of blacks in urban neighborhoods and schools, and the peaking and likely slow decline in the number of blacks holding elective office.

Beyond these oft-cited indicators of disparity in black-white opportunities are the actuarial costs of racial deprivation: blacks continue to have higher infant mortality and lower life expectancy rates than whites. And while they live, a disproportionately large percentage of those who are hungry and illiterate are black.

In the post-Reconstruction years, the promises of federal protection and land grants vanished in the dust of thundering lynch mobs. Contemporary remedies also avoid the direct, governmental subsidies that are the source of success for so much of American enterprise. Favored instead are spurious welfare-type measures that enable bare survival at the cost of pride, ambition, and a sense of self-achievement. The result can be seen in prison statistics, broken homes, illegitimate births, and such costly episodes of anti-social behavior as the looting of stores during the New York City power failure of July, 1977.

Compassion and belief are burdened by suggestions still made by well-meaning liberals that disadvantages under which blacks labor today are all the heritage of slavery. No group was ever so enslaved. Whatever other criticisms can be made about *Time On the Cross*, its authors were clearly correct in observing that "one of the worst consequences of the traditional interpretation of slavery is that it has diverted attention from the attack on the material conditions of black life that took place during the decades following the end of the Civil War."[81]

The Racial Imperative Revealed

All the previously discussed indicia of social disorganization and despair that plague so much of the black community are viewed by most of white America as evidence of at least the unreadiness of blacks for full citizenship, and perhaps as their inherent unworthiness for any important societal role. Contemporary social scientists, willing to follow their nineteenth-century predecessors, are able to reap fame and not an inconsiderable fortune by demonstrating talent in concocting biological or social science data into formulae somehow attributing to blacks responsibility for antisocial behavior that, in fact, is the consequence and not the cause of white exploitation.[82] It goes without saying that much of the populace accepts without question pseudoscientific proof that, by comparison, renders even the wildest science fiction plausible. In the condition of many blacks and the evaluation of the cause of those conditions by many whites, little has changed. The goals of the post–Civil War Redeemers remain the goals of today's Redeemed.

Can we conclude that judges sworn to defend the rights of individuals, and particularly the rights of racial minorities, render their decisions on a background that reflects agreement with the assessment of black inferiority espoused by some social scientists, and embraced so widely by the citizenry? Isn't it also likely that there are influences beyond recognition and personal profit that motivate policy-makers whether social scientists, historians, or judges? The desire—if not need—to function in phase with prevailing views and beliefs is very strong. This sense is epitomized by Justice Holmes's conclusion in *Giles* v. *Harris* that it was futile for the law to oppose even a violence-effected denial of basic citizenship rights if the masses support those violations. This is democratic totalitarianism exhibited with a vengeance, often touted but seldom tolerated in Socialist-run countries.

It is also, I suggest, an important component of the Racial Imperative. Recognition of the widely accepted if not very praiseworthy principle "to get along, go along" may well explain why courts and the law generally do not simply abandon enforcement of black rights entirely instead of alternately protecting, then ignoring, their duty to racial minorities. Here too is a rationale for the irrational perpetual dualism in the law's official recognition of, but periodic refusal to, protect the individual rights of not minorities alone, but any Americans whose views, like the early Vietnam War protestors, are threatening to policies the majority has concluded are necessary, if not right.

Historians are stalemated in the "chicken or the egg" type argument over whether the sense of black inferiority or the opportunity for profit led seventeenth-century whites to enslave blacks. Today, it is equally unclear whether what we define as racism reflects the continued belief in Caucasian superiority, or the reaction by whites to the sense of accusation that blacks by their very presense pose. But whatever generated slavery in America, the fact of slavery made the very presence of blacks thereafter a constant reminder of that dualism between moral principle so extolled in word, and the pragmatic, self-interest-oriented deed that so often tramples high-minded principle in hard-headed dust.[83]

The country's initial reaction to the Vietnam War protestors remains a useful analogy here. Imagine a minority group who, without using signs or shouting Vietcong slogans but simply by their presence, evokes a similar sense of unease and threat in the majority. It is not surprising that, experiencing this black-presence-induced unease, most whites react defensively, which, given their status vis-à-vis blacks, must be termed aggressively. This racial aggression is, I suggest, far more virulent because it must overcome, somehow, not only responsibility for enslaving blacks in a land consecrated to individual freedom, but also must wrestle with the fact that after slavery was abolished and the slaves made citizens, the country and its law imposed post-Reconstruction era agonies on the freedmen which, to paraphrase Chief Justice Warren in the *Brown* case, affected the hearts and minds of whites in America in a way unlikely ever to be undone.

This, then, is the Racial Imperative revealed. It is pervasive in the society and, because the law is an integral part of society, it is pervasive in the law. Its origins perhaps predate slavery, but its major thrust came during that period after 1876 when the country determined both that it would be too costly and, as we now see, too painful to carry out the commitments to black citizenship that political self-interest as well as abolitionist fervor had placed in the Constitution. What Rayford Logan describes as the nadir for blacks was also the nadir for whites. The wounds inflicted in those years by whites on whites have never healed because they have never been fully acknowledged. Gauging contemporary racial troubles by the experience of the half-century that began in 1890 requires the conclusion that the mandatory confession which must precede even the hope for a cure does not seem likely. If the televised version of Alex Haley's novel, *Roots*, is an accurate appraisal of how much of their past racial behavior most white Americans are ready to confront, no confession-preceded cure may be possible.[84]

Blacks, then, are condemned to bear the burdens and scars of past racial compromises: in 1660, when slavery was recognized by law; in 1787, when slavery was recognized in the Constitution; and in 1876 when their newly won citizenship rights were devalued into what might be called neoslavery. They must also face the threat, when political and economic conditions coincide, of present and future racial compromises. It is precisely that threat and not the words in the Constitution that define the lesser citizenship rights of black Americans. Future compromises, like those that have come before, will reflect specific concerns. They will be intended to protect special interests of a white majority that more than three hundred years after the first such "deal" continues—when things get rough—to view itself as white.

This willingness to surrender black rights to advance white interests is a principal characteristic of the unseen but powerful force which here is recognized and designated the Racial Imperative. Its origins lie in that moral schizophrenia that manifests itself in the country's deep but unspoken reliance on a dualism of principled thought and amoral, pragmatic action. In racial matters, moral duplicity is rendered easier to rationalize because of the continued need to believe, despite all contrary scientific evidence, that the humanity of blacks is somehow both different and less than that of whites.

Those who make and adjudicate American law understand and share this need. Until major sectors of the society perceive a real benefit to themselves, the chasm between promise and performance in racial policy-making in the courts, as elsewhere, will remain great and, measured by the mostly unpleasant precedents of the post-Reconstruction period, painfully familiar.

Repression of Blacks in the South 1890–1945: Enforcing the System of Segregation

MARY FRANCES BERRY

Black subordination in the South between 1890 and 1945 was made legal and generally supported by the federal government and northern whites. Segregation became the legal means of enforcement in a system devoted to the maintenance of white supremacy and black subordination. Poor people in the South, black and white, suffered economic oppression from the crop lien system, verbal contracts, and convict leases amounting to servitude, but racial segregation became a particular way of enforcing the subordination of blacks. Once segregation became legal, activity in opposition to it could easily be suppressed as illegal activity. Furthermore, prosegregationist church, newspaper and other opinion served to reinforce the legal status quo. Social institutions which operated to support segregation were operating routinely in conformity with law. Law in this case, whether seen as the expression of pre-existing views of right or wrong or as establishing a new system of social relations, was crucial. Therefore, understanding the process by which segregation became the legal means of enforcing the power status quo becomes most significant in any discussion of race relations in the South.

This paper discusses how and why segregation became the legal way of enforcing white supremacy and race control, and how the system of segregation was enforced as the legal means of maintaining white supremacy. In this context, violence, especially lynching, can be seen as an illegal means of enforcing black subordination. This illegal means would have been unnecessary if the legal means—segregation—had worked in all cases. Violence, then, became necessary despite the legal existence of segregation because segregation did not work in all cases. But violence could be a viable alternative means of enforcement only if its perpetrators were not so severely punished that it became too risky. The fact that those who controlled the legal system did not often punish illegal racial violence meant that it became for all intents and purposes a "legal" means of enforcing racial subordination when segregation did not work. When segregation, large-scale lynchings, and other forms of racial violence came to an end in the twentieth century, it was because whites did not regard such activities as necessary to the goal of maintaining white supremacy and black subordination. These means of enforcement had served their purposes and the economic oppression blacks had suffered since slavery ensured their continued subordination to whites without the necessity for the unsophisticated violence and overt racism of the pre–World War II period.

During the Reconstruction era, blacks achieved political rights and experienced a great deal of hope. The same military necessity which led to emancipation led to some political participation. During the period between Reconstruction and 1900, historians report that both segregation in public accommodations and integration occurred. But whether one regards law as the harbinger of things to come or the expression of what is, by 1900 legal segregation was the rule.[1]

The first precondition for the enactment of these laws was that those who desired them had the power to enact them. This power was achieved, in part, by disfranchising blacks. The disfranchisement occurred through the use of violence and intimidation, as a result of divisiveness among blacks, through taking advantage of blacks, and because of an absence of strong intervention by those who held power in the national government.[2]

In the aftermath of the Civil War, segregation instead of antebellum racial exclusion developed as southern policy toward blacks. Before the Civil War blacks were excluded from most military service and schools as well as hospitals, asylums, and public accommodations in the South. The state governments during Presidential Reconstruction attempted to maintain the exclusion. The United States Army and the Freedmen's Bureau forced the provision of schools for blacks, and during Congressional Reconstruction ensured the federal government the provision of public services for blacks. Republicans established separate black militia units, separate schools (except in Louisiana and South Carolina where integrated schools existed for a time), and separate welfare facilities for the care of the mute, blind, and deaf. Republicans, in general, enforced separate accommodations for blacks as a broad forward step from the policy of exclusion. This approach made logical sense. They were following the policy implemented for free and freed Negroes during the Civil War. This policy was a great reform for blacks and did not frighten whites as much as integration would have.[3]

The Republicans made little attempt to enforce the Civil Rights Act of 1875 which would have forced some integration, and the act was quickly declared unconstitutional in federal courts in Alabama, Richmond, and Savannah. Soon, of course, the Supreme Court declared it unconstitutional in 1883. When the southern Democrats took over state after state from Republicans, they continued segregation or attempted to exclude blacks again. Streetcars seemed to be an exception. There is some evidence that integration on streetcars resulted from the fact that with the horsecarts in use before 1880 a horse could pull only one cart at a time. Blacks could insist on integration because otherwise they could walk, use hacks, or take private carriages.[4]

Blacks protested segregation but sometimes supported it for economic reasons. This had also been the case in the antebellum period; black barbers would refuse to service blacks for fear of losing their white clientele. When black protests against segregation failed, they insisted on separate but equal facilities instead of exclusion. By 1890, segregation was more prevalent as racial policy in the South than exclusion. Whites legalized segregation only to make it a permanent, prominent policy and to make it possible to punish, within the law, violations of it. The disfranchisement of blacks permitted the whites to vote segregation into law.[5]

Courts, Congress, and chief executives were responsible for the political process of legalizing segregation. The Supreme Court had declared segregated public accommodations legal in 1883 and had refused to implement Reconstruction legislation designed to suppress violence against blacks who attempted to vote because the acts were interpreted to apply only to state and not individual action. By 1896, the Court had put the stamp of approval on separate but equal in *Plessy* v. *Ferguson,* and the Interstate Commerce Commission, established in 1887, had ruled that Jim Crow laws imposed no undue burden on black passengers.[6]

The Congress passed no civil rights legislation after the Supreme Court's 1883 decision declaring the Civil Rights Act of 1875 unconstitutional. In 1890, the Congress considered Henry Lodge's election bill, which provided for federal supervisors to inspect registration books, attend elections, and certify the results. The bill, passed in the House by a strict party line vote, died in a Senate committee. Liberal Republican opponents of the bill insisted that education was the answer to the race problem. Once blacks were educated they would be permitted to vote in the South. If those Republicans were correct, the failure of the Congress that same year to pass the Blair Bill, which would provide federal aid to education, and the failure of state governments to educate blacks were not helpful to the ultimate goal.[7]

Presidents of the United States and their subordinates in the executive branch abandoned efforts to enforce civil rights laws or to set a tone of moral leadership after Rutherford Hayes's election in 1877. The Republican party left blacks to be controlled by local whites, tried to establish a lily white southern wing of the party and to reconcile the sections by taking a hands-off policy where blacks were concerned, and refused to use federal troops to protect black citizens from violence and intimidation.[8]

In some southern states, South Carolina, North Carolina, and Louisiana in particular, some blacks shared political power with whites during Reconstruction and for a period thereafter. But, without national support and divided internally along class lines, they soon lost to whites even the meager opportunities open to them.[9]

Violence, night riders, and Red Shirts, divisiveness in the black community and federal withdrawal of support had aided the efforts of the Democrats in the South to wrest political control from the Republicans. Economic oppression had aided the Democrats in gaining political control. Radical agrarian movements in the South were the basis of a resurgence of black political activity in the 1890s, but conservatives drove a wedge between poor blacks and whites and gained the alliance of poor whites in disfranchising blacks. Whites understood that if blacks could vote and whites were divided, then blacks would have the balance of power. Reading and understanding clauses and grandfather clauses were the instruments of disfranchisement. Once disfranchisement was accomplished, the legalization of white supremacy was possible.[10]

` Beyond the logical reasons for the institution of segregation by Republicans and Redeemers, segregation had a great deal of philosophical appeal to the white South. Before the Civil War most whites asserted that blacks, even free Negroes, were an inferior race to be kept under control by white society. The military necessity of the Civil War did not change these views about blacks. In the North after the war, blacks remained victims of discrimination and social and economic oppression. In any event, the alternative of the complete exclusion of blacks from public services was not available to white southerners because the Republicans had moved toward segregation, and the reimposition of exclusion everywhere would have required forcible execution. Organized force was expensive and unnecessary if segregation could achieve the desired effect.[11]

Those southerners who gained power after Reconstruction and implemented segregation extended the theory of paternalism developed under slavery to the notion that blacks needed the protection of whites as they developed. The most advanced thinking of those who developed the paternalists' philosophy— such as Lewis H. Blair, born of Virginia planter aristocracy, and Bishop T. V. Dudley of the Protestant Episcopal Church in Kentucky—reflected a belief that blacks needed only educational and economic opportunities to advance. Some whites believed just as emphatically in uplift, but thought blacks would never be equal to whites but could learn to become good citizens and productive workers. Some of these opposed the Rosenwald, Peabody, and Slater funds for not giving blacks the proper kind of education. Booker T. Washington, in his advocacy of industrial education, became a natural leader for this group.[12]

Southern white understanding of the nature and role of blacks was shared by whites in the North. Throughout the period from the Civil War to the 1920s, northern newspapers, magazines, and plays justified segregation and the subordination of blacks. News writers approved of lynching and showed blacks as stupid, morally degraded, and inferior. A favorite newspaper stereotype was the "burly" criminal Negro who was often a "ruffian" or a "cannibal." Playwrights described blacks as irrepressibly happy,

instinctively servile and loyal to whites, cowardly, morally de-
based, unintelligent, given to drunkenness and the theft of water-
melons, pigs, and chickens (which were their preferred diet),
and prone to fighting with razors amidst incessant petty quar-
reling. Black participation in politics, according to the writers,
meant corruption, and black migration to the cities caused
degeneracy and riots. The playwright mirrored and reflected the
attitudes of businessmen, teachers, editors, and other opinion-
makers and molders. These writers helped to heal the nation
after the Civil War by creating a nostalgic view of a vanished
noble civilization. The plantation in their hands was a grand
estate ruled over by a benevolent despot who displayed an
always paternal interest in his slaves. It did not matter that the
images created by the artists existed only in exceptional circumstances. The public applauded the depiction of this dimly re-
membered past and accepted the exaggerated portrait of the
plantation as truth.[13]

Because each southern plantation as described by the writers
had hundreds of slaves, blacks found a place in the stories. The
portrayal of slaves was no more real than the mythologized setting in which they were placed, but the black slaves played
standardized roles—the very epitome of loyalty and devotion,
willing to go to any length to insure the safety and security of
their white folks. Slaves showed remarkable contentment with
their subordinate status. They rejected freedom when it was
offered, preferring to remain on the plantation in voluntary
servitude. In the event that they accepted emancipation, they
either became extremely successful, often returning to visit the
old plantation with affection, or if unsuccessful lived to regret
the choice of freedom and longed for the more comfortable life
of slavery. Rarely, if ever, did the slaves' attitude reflect any
animosity toward the old master. Instead, they showed deep
gratitude for all he had done for them. Because slaves were always humorous creatures, they elicited great mirth from audi-

ences in their attempts to mimic white culture. They were, of course, incredibly ignorant but deeply devoted to emulating the behavior of the master. Even when slaves migrated to the city following emancipation, far from being allowed to become respectable citizens, they slipped down into the most sordid type of life. Blacks who lived decently and quietly, earnestly attempting to overcome the handicap of their previous condition, had not the slightest attraction for either the playwrights or the public. Writers such as Albion Tourgee and George Washington Cable, who wrote more objectively and favorably about the black situation, were a distinctly small minority.[14]

Minstrel shows, begun in the 1840s, remained after the war a most popular form of entertainment. Performed by whites in black face before the war, they presented images of blacks shaped by white expectations and not by reality. When blacks began performing minstrel shows after the war, to gain acceptance, they were restricted to the caricatures that had been long performed by whites. When blacks were not portrayed as docile old darkies nostalgically remembering the happy days of youth in slavery, they became ridiculous "coons."[15]

As in the minstrel shows, whites played the roles of blacks in the theatre for much of the late nineteenth century. When blacks such as Bert Williams were finally permitted to play themselves in the early twentieth century, they played the roles already made traditional. Williams played the mentally retarded, lazy, uneducated Negro who always managed to find a way to make even the best laid plans go awry. With the beginning of motion picture films, blacks found themselves in the same unfavorable position. Beginning with *Uncle Tom's Cabin* in 1903, whites in black face played the roles and developed the traditional caricatures. When blacks began playing these roles they were wedged into these same familiar categories of coons, mammies, and Toms. Not until the 1940s did blacks begin to play a wider variety of roles than jesters and servants.[16]

The uses to which scientific theory was put in the late nineteenth and early twentieth centuries led to worse results for blacks than those achieved by the playwrights. When Darwin used a subtitle "The Preservation of Favored Races in the Struggle for Life" for his *The Origin of Species* in 1859, he was not referring to human beings, but that did not prevent others from using his theories for different purposes. If only the fittest animals survived in evolution, then of course the less fit, inferior human beings, such as blacks, would lose out in the evolutionary competition. By 1915 the reform economist John Commons could seriously assert: "Race differences are established in the very blood and physical constitution. They are most difficult to eradicate, and they yield only to the slow processes of the centuries." In the meantime, while these race differences existed, they provided a convenient rationale for colonial expansion.[17]

Scientific theories of race differences and superiority among human beings provided fertile ground for the flourishing of imperialist ideas in the United States. America's imperialistic ventures could be rationalized in terms of ersatz Darwinism, but the ventures could in turn rationalize the oppression of blacks in this country. The United States purchased Alaska in 1867 and tried unsuccessfully to annex Santo Domingo in the 1870s. The Europeans provided additional encouragement by their rapid colonization of Africa, completed by the partitioning of the continent in 1884. Their example inspired historian John Fiske's lecture on Manifest Destiny published in 1885 and Protestant clergyman Josiah Strong's book of the same year in which he asserted that the "Anglo-Saxon race" was destined to "spread itself all over the earth" and the result, of course, would be the "survival of the fittest" in competition with the indigenous weaker races.[18]

Americans gave their attention to expansion to the west and south. America overthrew the Hawaiian government in 1893 and the islands were annexed by the United States in 1898. The United States supported the Cuban Revolution in 1895 and used the destruction of the *Maine* in Havana harbor as a pretext for war against Spain in 1898. In the six-month Spanish-American War, Cuba, Puerto Rico, and the Philippines became American colonial possessions. Between 1904 and 1944, the United States continually intervened or occupied Haiti and the Dominican Republic as if they were American colonies. The nonwhites who occupied these colonized lands, like blacks in the United States, were regarded as examples of perfectly stupid races who could not govern themselves. Therefore, whites must take on the burden of controlling and developing these lands and the nonwhites who lived in them. Undertaking this burden would, according to Lothrop Stoddard, extend and "fortify white race consciousness with its sanctions," because all of civilization is and must be the product of the "white man's brain."[19]

The objective of extending the white man's burden by Europeans and white Americans was definitely not intermarriage and race-mixing. Even though, arguably, the children of mixed blood would be much improved over the nonwhite races from which they partially sprang, instead, according to one writer: "We must substitute definitely organized cooperation for fusion and intermixture. The specific characters of races must be brought into account and differential functions be sought. The failure of the isolated negro in Liberia and Haiti shows that a better way for the negro is for him to take advantage of his capacity for working along with others and to find for himself a place in a wider industrial and social order, higher in kind than he could himself devise or maintain." Indeed he believed that such an approach "is the line advocated by leaders of the Negro race in the United States."[20]

In this congenial atmosphere, white oppression of blacks reached a fully developed stage. When the unification effort of the Populists in the early 1890s failed, the farmers who gained control of the southern state governments became virulent racist demagogues. They appealed to the basest emotions of their constituents. From 1890 to 1920 white supremacy became the major issue for southern politicians. To such arrant racists as Governor James K. Vardaman of Mississippi, and Governor Cole Blease and Senator "Pitchfork" Ben Tillman of South Carolina, blacks, unlike normal human beings, were incapable of improvement. In this setting, southern white moderates like George Washington Cable and Edgar Gardner Murphy were overwhelmed by the pure racists. Northerners were little better. William Jennings Bryan, the perennial presidential candidate, believed that white supremacy and the disfranchisement of blacks were "absolutely essential to the welfare of the youth." Most of the so-called Social Gospelists and Progressives ignored blacks, and even when they did not they generally were enlightened racists of the Murphy type. In 1914 Walter Rauschenbusch, the foremost Social Gospelist, believed that whites needed to take blacks by the hand and lead them to further development. The most radical of the white progressives who could not stomach racism gave their support to the organization of the NAACP.[21]

Throughout the nineteenth and early twentieth centuries, scientists in England and the United States tried persistently to prove that blacks were intellectually inferior to whites in conformity with "Darwinism." While nineteenth-century scientists measured skulls to show that the brains of blacks weighed less than those of whites, during the twentieth century the scientists turned increasingly to genetics. After the Frenchman Alfred Binet developed a test in 1905 that allegedly predicted success in school, Americans quickly adopted it as a measure of intelligence. When these tests showed lower scores for blacks and the foreign-born, scientists contended these groups were inferior. The scores were used to restrict immigration of southern Europeans, Asians, and Africans to America and to support the necessity for inferior segregated schools and limited employment opportunities for blacks. Anthropologist Franz Boas, who challenged the main currents in his work, did not stem the tide. Comparative mental measurements of whites and blacks rapidly became a fully developed specialty in psychology. A test of black and white Philadelphia children led a researcher to conclude, incidentally without statistical evidence, that "colored pupils as a class were good in the memory tests and poor in those requiring judgment." Another researcher found that the upper social class Negroes stood about midway between the whites and the poor Negro group. The author suggested that "the Negroes composing the upper social class may have more white blood than the others." His finding was confirmed by another colleague who "being accustomed to Negroes, classified his subjects into full blooded, three-quarters, mulatto, and quadroon on the basis of color, hair, and features." He reached the "clear" result that success increased with the proportion of white blood."[22]

By 1925 the Binet individual test and Lewis Terman's Stanford revision of it were being displaced by the use of the group intelligence test developed since the introduction of the Otis test and the widespread use of the army group tests. Intelligence quotient tests were also used increasingly. Researchers using each available test reported what they regarded as a positive correlation between the scores received and the degree of white blood possessed by a Negro subject. But the most impressive "proof" of black inferiority was the results of army tests given to the men drafted in World War I. Analysts found again that black soldiers scored much lower than whites and concluded that blacks were genetically inferior to whites in intelligence. But more intensive studies showed that northern blacks had scored higher than southern whites which, of course, meant that either southern whites were genetically inferior to northern blacks or some factor other than genetics had significance for the subject. Additionally, work evolving from this finding helped to advance the flight of the hereditarian racist social scientists. World War II and Hitler's attempt to exterminate Jews who were "inferior" by his standards helped the liberal environmentalists to capture social science discussion of the issue. Not until white fears that blacks would gain improved economic status at their expense became endemic in the 1970s did the hereditarian racists again gain a hearing in the ranks of social science scholars.[23]

Once the political, social, and cultural evolution of segregation is understood, lynching and racial violence may be seen in the context of the enforcement of the subordination of blacks in the period between 1890 and 1945. At first, lynching and violence were necessary only when blacks violated the segregation rules designed to insure their subordination to whites. Interracial contacts and black militancy were the major crises for which lynching became the remedy. But illegal murder and assault worked only because its perpetrators escaped with slight or no punishment. Lynching was a quite popular mode of exacting quick illegal punishment in the late nineteenth century. Between 1882 and 1935 there were about 5,053 reported lynchings in the United States; most of them occurred in the South and an overwhelming majority of the victims were black.[24]

A great deal of racial violence and lynching was related to reports that blacks had assaulted white women, to militancy by blacks who opposed segregation, to strikes and other efforts by blacks to improve their economic condition in opposition to peonage and unequal contracts, and to efforts to end black political activity. In the twentieth century the racial violence in connection with political activity largely dissipated. Of those activities that led to lynchings many occurred because of faults in the wall of segregation that had been established. If legal segregation had eliminated all black militancy and interracial contracts, the illegal violence would not have been necessary.

For all intents and purposes the violence was also legal. Rarely were whites prosecuted for the illegal murder of blacks. State and local governments did not punish the killers, and federal governmental officials insisted throughout the period that murder was not a federal crime.[25]

Black organizations protested against illegal violence throughout the late nineteenth and early twentieth centuries. They were increasingly supported by some whites north and south. After the NAACP was organized in 1908, a federal antilynching law became a major goal of the organization. Three times—in 1922, 1937, and 1940—an antilynching bill was passed in the House but failed of passage in the Senate. Still, by 1945 no antilynching law had been passed. By that time, however, the frequency of lynching had diminished. Publicity about the issue and the race-based causes of its occurrence, and the new negative public attitude about racism and hereditarianism engendered by opposition to the Nazis, helped to make lynchings less frequent. Additionally, the movement of large numbers of blacks to northern cities, where they voted and soon became an important political factor, led politicians and presidents to begin publicly voicing opposition to lynching.[26]

These same factors led to increasing success for the NAACP and other black individuals and organizations in obtaining legal opinions that began assaulting segregation. By the end of World War II, the doctrine that facilities that were separate could be equal was increasingly accepted as a legal principle. The end of segregation awaited further development in law and national policy after the war. The contradictions in America's professed belief in equality and the subordination of blacks were made too obvious by the paradox of fighting a world war for democracy against an enemy supporting a master race ideology while upholding white supremacy at home.[27] The international politics of post–World War II America made the successes of the civil rights movement in the 1950s and 1960s possible. An end to segregation was in view but not an end to the subordination of blacks. The economic legacy of slavery made it possible for whites to face an end to legal segregation without conceding an end to their preferred economic position over blacks. Continued economic oppression in contemporary America requires legal theories which affirm the existence of an equal chance for blacks and ascribes their continued inferior status to their own inadequate motivation or intelligence. For these theories, reverse discrimination and genetic causes are more adequate weapons than legal segregation and its illegal partner, lynching.

Southern Political Style

DAN CARTER

In the fall of 1949, Ralph McGill confidently looked forward to the first full-scale political campaign that would follow the legal destruction of the white Democratic primary in the South. With the number of black voters increasing dramatically, the editor of the Atlanta *Constitution* predicted basic changes in the politics of the South. Competition for the Negro vote was "already a fact in the states of the old Confederacy," said McGill. In the brief period after the Supreme Court's decision in *Smith* v. *Allwright*, this changed political climate had paved streets in black neighborhoods, "put Negro police in uniform, established Negro fire stations, put Negroes in minor elective offices, equalized some school salaries, built new schools and constructed parks and playgrounds."[1]

The optimism of McGill was based upon two observations. In his own city of Atlanta, white politicians had begun to openly appeal to blacks, and throughout the South the number of black voters had quadrupled in three years—from less than 150,000 to more than 600,000. While the majority of this increase came in the border states and the region's largest metropolitan cities, every southern state except South Carolina, Alabama, and Mississippi reported significant gains.[2]

The following year, however, southerners experienced one of

45

the most racially dominated series of political campaigns in the twentieth century. In Florida, George Smathers turned on his old mentor, Claude Pepper, with a savage blend of new-style McCarthyism and old-style racism. Early in the campaign he had dubbed his opponent the "Red Pepper" and repeatedly linked the New Deal–Fair Deal senator with Communist front organizations and any group which smacked of "un-American socialism." During the campaign, Smathers's supporters published a vicious pamphlet entitled "The Red Record of Senator Claude Pepper" that was scurrilous even by the rather lax standards of the early 1950s. This was also the campaign where Smathers allegedly made use of the explosive charge that Pepper's wife had been a practicing "thespian" before their marriage; that his father was a self-acknowledged "philatelist"; and that the Florida senator himself was a well-known heterosexual who practiced celibacy before his marriage.[3]

But it was the race issue which proved most effective. Defensively, Pepper insisted that he had not backed the Fair Employment Practices Committee and the Truman administration's assault on the southern way of life. With increasing vigor he insisted that he supported segregation "now and forever." Smathers simply responded by hammering away at Pepper as a tool of the NAACP and a captive of the black vote. Despite capturing 90 percent of that vote, Pepper went down to decisive defeat.[4]

The race issue was even more clearly drawn in the North Carolina senatorial primary which pitted the liberal incumbent Frank Graham against conservative corporation lawyer Willis Smith. In the June, 1950, runoff between the two, Smith piously insisted that the "black bloc vote" should not be an issue in the campaign, while his supporters poured from anonymous printing presses handbills and leaflets which claimed Graham supported miscegenation and advocated replacing white workers with "black bucks and wenches." The vote was closer than in Florida, but Smith, the former president of the University of North Carolina, went down to defeat.[5]

In the South Carolina senatorial campaign of that year, the two main candidates were Governor Strom Thurmond and incumbent Olin D. Johnston. Unlike Frank Graham and Claude Pepper, neither could by any stretch of the imagination be described as "soft" on Communists or blacks. Nevertheless, the race question dominated speechmaking as each tried to hang his opponent with the albatross of black political support. As the June runoff drew to a close, Thurmond and Johnston took to the hustings in a series of open debates throughout the state. In Walterboro, with a black contingent seated in the Jim Crow gallery, Johnston launched into a long summation of his attempts as governor to maintain the sanctity of the white ballot box. His remarks brought forth derisive and angry shouts from the black spectators. Thurmond, not to be outdone, responded by noting Johnston's endorsement of the "pro communist, pro-integration" Democratic platform of 1948. He compared this with his own commitment as governor and Dixiecrat candidate to see to it that no Negro children defiled the purity of South Carolina's white classrooms. At that point, black members of the audience began emitting catcalls, and an excited—and obviously pleased —Thurmond ran to the front of the stage: "See, see," he shouted, "they're hissing and booing me more than they did him." While Johnston retained his seat, it was hardly the kind of elevating campaign Ralph McGill had in mind when he predicted a new era in southern politics.[6]

It is unfair to criticize the late Mr. McGill for his flawed prophecy without pointing to the importance of southern blacks in electing a Georgia cracker as president in 1976. If his predictions went awry by a quarter century, that is still a better track record than most journalistic political pundits. Nevertheless, the political campaigns of 1950 are worth noting for the speedy epitaph they wrote to the premature hopes of McGill and his fellow "liberal" southerners who believed the abolition of the white Democratic primary would de-escalate the political rhetoric of southern racism. What is more important, these campaigns reflect the remarkable strength and continuity of the race question in southern politics. Despite the social and economic changes that had reshaped southern society in the first half of the twentieth century, the racial shibboleths which dominated the era of Teddy Roosevelt and Woodrow Wilson remained to haunt those southerners who lived in the age of the atom.

The factors which underlie this continuity are many. We cannot hope to unravel them at once, but a brief look at the style—and some of the substance—of twentieth-century southern politics may help to explain the tenacity with which white southerners fought against extending the most elementary rights in a democratic society.

While race consciousness was the most potent political factor in the three decades after the Civil War, the particular political rhetoric of twentieth-century race relations was established in the wake of the disfranchisement campaigns of the 1890s. As C. Vann Woodward noted nearly three decades ago, the proponents of disfranchisement had insisted that the removal of the Negro from politics would lead to a decline in racial conflicts.[7] Race would cease to be the violently divisive issue it had been since the 1860s. The bitter irony of southern political history is that disfranchisement simply set the stage for a new and far more brutal chapter.

With some notable exceptions, there were relatively few political campaigns in the 1880s when white politicians—conservative, radical, or liberal—publicly opposed black political participation in principle. Since the Black Belt Democratic conservatives were most successful in gaining the support of black voters, they were understandably reluctant to give up this electoral bonus. In Mississippi, for example, the Jackson *Clarion* repeatedly endorsed Negro suffrage between 1875 and 1888.[8] And even though upcountry dissident Democrats were less enthusiastic over the spectacle of black voters casting Democratic ballots, criticism of black political activity was almost always couched in terms of opposition to specific leaders and policies. In 1878 Elbridge Gary, Ben Tillman's political godfather, pushed through a resolution in Edgefield County, South Carolina, barring Negro voters from participating in the primaries of that county. Other upcountry conventions quickly rushed to condemn the Edgefield Democrats. Such political proscription would sink South Carolina "to the level of a half-civilized people," declared a neighboring newspaper editor. Democratic conventions in five upcountry counties specifically condemned the Edgefield resolution; none supported it.[9]

This tender concern for the political rights of southern blacks stemmed from a number of nonaltruistic motives. White southerners still feared federal intervention to protect black voting rights. Conservative Democrats saw no reason to abandon black voters when they posed little threat and offered significant assistance in crucial elections. And upcountry and piedmont dissidents feared (rightly it now appears) that disfranchisement might be applied along class as well as racial lines. Whatever the motivation, the political rights of black southerners were often defended in principle even as they were violated in practice.[10]

Such political tolerance had come to an end by the close of the nineteenth century. It is instructive to look at the career of those white southerners who, from many different perspectives, defended the political rights of blacks in the 1880s. In 1886, George Washington Cable attempted to establish an "Open Letter Club" of white southerners opposed to political, legal, and economic discrimination against blacks. Despite an initially encouraging response, his correspondence reflected a marked shift after 1890. Robert T. Hill, a southern-born geologist who left the coast and geodetic survey in the mid-1880s to teach at the University of Texas, kept Cable informed of his successes in finding the "silent" southerners who defended the rights of blacks. By the 1890s, however, Hill wrote Cable that he had been forced to cease all discussion on the issue of black political rights: "If I open my mouth it means decapitation, and the warning axe hangs ready." Cable himself had to leave the South. For most other southern whites who had defended black political rights, silence or a public recantation of their earlier heresy was the practice as the twentieth century began. The handful of white heretics who had defended black political rights in the 1890s acted from a variety of motives: paternalism, political "realism," or simply an open-minded attitude on the question. By the end of the first decade of the twentieth century, this group was nonexistent in southern society.[11]

The absence of any countervailing force from within the South or from the rest of the nation removed the last major obstacles to the emergence of virulent and unabashed racism in southern politics. Thus in the first three decades of the twentieth century, a new group of southern politicians emerged —the southern demagogues. While violent racism formed the core of their appeal, they were able to tap many forms of fear and hatred within the white southern electorate. Simply to list their names is to summon a host of vivid, sometimes comic, sometimes sinister, images: James K. Vardaman, "Pitchfork Ben" Tillman, Tom Watson, Theodore Bilbo, Jeff Davis, Cole Blease, Ellison D. ("Cotton Ed") Smith, Huey ("the Kingfish") Long, Eugene Talmadge, "Tom Tom" Heflin, "Pa" Ferguson, W. E. ("Pass the Biscuits, Pappy") O'Daniel.

Their flamboyant campaign styles alone have been enough to capture the imaginations and attention of contemporaries and historians. In the late 1890s, James K. Vardaman, the "Great White Chief" of Greenwood, Mississippi, had set a mark to which all his successors might aspire as he campaigned across the state from the back of an ox-drawn cart, dressed in a spotless white suit, wearing a cowboy hat over his long, black, flowing hair. As the acerbic Walker Alexander Percy cynically concluded, he would have made a damn fine impresario for a medicine show.[12]

Cotton Ed Smith of South Carolina was only a trifle less flamboyant during his campaigns for the United States Senate. According to one story, he had launched his 1907 senatorial campaign by entering the town square of Darlington on a mule-drawn wagon. There he perched upon five bales of cotton. Behind him, a grizzled old dirt farmer bowed his head in mute adoration; another of Smith's supporters knelt in gratitude while Cotton Ed stroked the white-tipped bud of the cotton boll in his lapel and declaimed loudly, "My sweetheart! My sweetheart! Others may forget you, but you will always be my sweetheart!"[13]

But they were more than showmen; they breathed a kind of electric vitality which shocked and fascinated genteel Americans. Their campaign rhetoric was the language of the frontier—a billingsgate of invective and slander which never ceased to delight and excite their followers. Mississippi's own James K. Vardaman was a master of such verbal abuse. An opponent was never simply an unscrupulous fool, he was a "scurvy biped without courage, conscience or conviction," a "moral pervert and cowardly liar," an "irresponsible and unscrupulous cur fit only for things filthy," a "scoundrel without the virtue of courage," an "assassin of character . . . who would strike you in the dark and then hide his cancerous carcass to avoid the just punishment which his damnable deeds deserve."[14]

Vardaman's political heir, Theodore Bilbo, raised such flights of rhetoric to new heights (or depths) as he labeled editor Frederick Sullens of the Jackson *Daily News* a "degenerate by birth, a carpetbagger by inheritance, a liar by instinct, a slanderer and assassin of character by practice, and a coward by nature."[15] On one occasion, Bilbo misjudged the patience—and physical prowess—of his opponent Ross Collins by describing him as the "offspring of a hyena and a mongrel, begotten in a graveyard at midnight, suckled by a sow and educated by a damn fool." Bilbo went to his grave with the scars of the pistol-whipping he endured at the hands of Collins.[16]

Such antics, however, hardly explain the interest of contemporaries and later historians. We return again and again to the so-called demagogues because they so skillfully roamed the unsettling terrain of white southern thought and orchestrated the themes of racism, regionalism, and a half-formed class hatred and resentment. The siege mentality of white southerners was not a creation of these demagogues; they simply capitalized upon a white folklore which had long emphasized a heritage of regional persecution and abuse. It is no accident that the mythology of Radical Reconstruction—the absurd notion that the South underwent a nightmare of rape and plunder from 1867 to 1877—was forged in the very period that political white supremacy reached its apogee. The lurid and inflammatory exaggerations of the Reconstruction became a historical object lesson that exemplified the dangers of granting political rights to black southerners. In its essential outlines, it was a mythology ultimately shared by most southerners, rich and poor, educated and illiterate, even black as well as white.[17]

Any northern challenge of southern mores (particularly on the race question) became the basis for impassioned speeches on the horrors of Yankee intervention. When Theodore Roosevelt tried to retain a black postmistress in Mississippi his action brought forth a stream of calumny from every politician in the state, conservative or moderate, demagogic or restrained.[18]

It was the blend of regional grievances and the manipulation of racial issues that came to characterize the southern "demagogues" in the minds of most Americans. When Booker T. Washington dined at the White House with President Roosevelt in 1902, Vardaman told his audiences he did not care how many "coons" Teddy took to the White House: "I should not care if

the walls of that ancient edifice should become so saturated with
the effluvia from their rancid carcasses that a chinch bug would
have to crawl upon the dome to avoid asphyxiation." According
to one native-born Mississippian who watched in horror, Vardaman's 1903 campaign for the governorship was marked by the
kind of racial venom which "for low-down vulgarity and in-
decency" exceeded anything that had ever fallen from the lips
of a public man.[19] Thirty-five years later, Eugene Talmadge, the
wild man from Sugar Creek, Georgia, exploded with anger at
the sight of Eleanor Roosevelt attending a Howard University
graduation, or as Talmadge put it, attending some "nigger meet-
ing with a nigger escort on each arm."[20] Between the two
episodes, a thousand political campaigns would pass in which
unbridled racial venom would dominate the rhetoric of southern
politics. The fastidious William Alexander Percy might rail
against the Vardamans and the Bilbos—the "slick little bastards"
who had appealed to the "sort of people that lynch Negroes, that
mistake hoodlumism for wit and cunning for intelligence, that
attend revivals and fight and fornicate in the bushes after-
wards."[21] But the success of the Great White Chief and his
spiritual heirs reflected a series of deep and fearful currents in
the thinking of white southerners.

During the depression years, the heightened consciousness of
class divisions in American society and the rise of European
fascism led a number of journalists to argue that southern demagogues were proto-fascists reshaping the class hatred they had
always employed into an instrument that would allow the growth
of fascist dictatorships. Under such catchy titles as "Fascism,
American Style," "Tarheel Fuehrer," "Red Gallused Hitler," and
"Master of the Masses," journalists warned of the imminent
danger to the Republic posed by the southern demagogues.[22]

The "class conflict" which writers of the 1930s uncovered was
simply a new variation of a very old tune. The hearty contempt
of the southern rich and the southern poor for each other had

been concealed at times by racial solidarity or the etiquette of deference, but some form of class consciousness has existed throughout southern history. Southern "gentlemen" from William Byrd to William Alexander Percy made clear their disdain for the white southern masses. And the poor, while usually less literarily articulate, often reciprocated at the ballot box.[23] Taken together, however, such class tension within the society was hardly the stuff to form a fascist movement. Somehow it was difficult to envision Cotton Ed Smith engineering a "Reichstag" fire or Tom Tom Heflin staging a Beer Hall putsch. Huey Long, the most successful of the southern political mass leaders, was able to overwhelm his political opponents, but even Long was unable to eradicate dissent within his own state, let alone the rest of the nation.[24]

The very ease with which journalists transformed southern rabble-rousers into potential Hitlers or Mussolinis raises serious questions about this popular perception of southern politics. Some time ago, George Tindall reviewed the corruption of the term "populist" and expressed reservations about any label that had been used to encompass politicians from Bella Abzug to George Wallace.[25] Much the same could be said about the use of the term "demagogue" to describe these southern politicians. As late as 1955, historian Reinhard Luthin tried manfully to breathe some life into this concept in his study of American demagogues in the twentieth century. Such demagogues, North and South, were "insincere" and manipulative figures, said Luthin, who cynically used racial, religious, and class hatreds to achieve power. Once in office, however, they showed a complete lack of concern for any interest except their own.[26]

Luthin's selection of biographical subjects almost immediately raises questions. For what are we to make of an analytical term which embraces New York's leftist congressman Vito Marcantonio and Georgia's Eugene Talmadge? At the same time, even the most cursory review of the careers of the so-called southern demagogues reveals the limitations of Luthin's descriptive framework. The social vision of Cole Blease of South Carolina seems to have extended no further than his desire to obtain a comfortable sinecure which would allow him to pardon a gaggle of convicted felons and entertain his cronies at someone else's expense. But, while James K. Vardaman and Theodore Bilbo aroused race and class hatred, they used the powers of their offices aggressively to protect the interests of the poorer farmers who had elected them. And there were substantial differences even between Vardaman and Bilbo. Bilbo shamelessly exploited anti-Semitism and anti-Catholicism with repeated references to "dagoes" and "kikes." Although it should be noted that Bilbo denied that he was anti-Semitic, in one memorable speech in Leland, Mississippi, in 1946, he declared that he was a friend of "every damn Jew from Jesus Christ on down." Vardaman, on the other hand, generally ignored the Catholic issue and vehemently defended Jews from the slanders of anti-Semites.[27]

More than a decade ago, Professor T. Harry Williams recognized the limitations of the traditional definitions of southern demagoguery and sought to use a different approach to understanding these men. Drawing upon the writings of Eric Hoffer, he argued that the term "mass leader" might be more appropriate. The mass leader should have "audacity, an iron will, faith in himself and his cause and his destiny, a recognition that the innermost craving of a following is for 'communion' or a sense of collectivity, unbounded brazenness, which enables the leader to disregard consistency, and a capacity for hatred." The good mass leaders—the Lincolns, the Gandhis, the Roosevelts—harness man's fears and hungers to a just cause. The bad ones—the Hitlers, the Stalins—use the frustration of man to build a nightmarish "brave new world."[28]

I'm not sure what such abstract comments have to do with the so-called southern demagogues. Some were genuinely mass leaders—Huey Long and Tom Watson, for example—while others were political clowns and entertainers who desperately sought the support of their fellow southerners and often failed to find it. There is nothing more pathetic than the last years of Cole Blease or North Carolina's Bob Reynolds as they sought to regain the support of an electorate which had tired of their antics and tirades.

The more closely one examines these so-called demagogues, the more elusive becomes the consistent generalization which will encompass all of them. The aggressive use of racist rhetoric is perhaps the hallmark of the southern demagogue. (And here I exclude Huey Long. He was, as he said on many occasions, *sui generis*.) Even here, however, we may be talking about differences in style rather than substance.

The civilizing restraints of paternalism, the imperatives of a Christian conscience, the natural restraint of a gentleman—these factors might act to temper the rhetoric of southern politicians, but they seldom furnished the intellectual framework for a substantive challenge to the effects of white supremacy, let alone its basic assumptions. Certainly it made a difference to a black South Carolinian if a race-baiting Cole Blease or a humane and progressive Richard Manning sat in the governor's chair. Nevertheless, there were inherent limitations placed on the actions of every southern politician. The final hardening of social segregation and political disfranchisement in the 1890s had created, in the minds of most white southerners, a seamless fabric of many strands. Some were rational, some irrational, some relatively harmless, others unspeakably cruel. To pull at one strand, however, was to risk unraveling the entire garment with unacceptable consequences. This meant that any subject— no matter how marginally involved with the structure of white supremacy—could become subject to the racial imperatives of southern thought.[29]

Of course racism was not restricted to the South. Color consciousness existed throughout the nation and had been height-

ened by the growing migration of blacks to the northern cities
of the nation in the first two decades of the twentieth century.
It was in Chicago and east St. Louis as well as Atlanta that race
riots occurred between 1900 and 1920. Blacks, however, were
able to establish their civil and political rights without serious
challenge outside the South. As Robert Wiebe has observed in
his study, *The Segmented Society,* in a complex, urban, industrial
society, Jim Crow laws are an anachronism. Homes and schools
—particularly for the middle and upper classes—are insulated
by geography. And occupational security, safely segregated, was
the real key to success; access to the ballot box was a subsidiary
road to significant power. Under these circumstances, legal
segregation above all "seemed absurd."[30]

In important respects, Wiebe's observations echo those of
recent historians of "modernization." In a "modernizing" society,
changes in the economic structure of society lead to a basic shift
in social values. The traditional "static" values that characterized
the Old South—honor, community loyalty, strong family ties,
deference—were basically at odds with those of the changing
order. The rigid apartheid of the twentieth-century South was a
direct affront to the goals of rationality, specialization, efficiency,
and cosmopolitanism which supposedly characterized a modern
society.[31]

And there can be little question that the South, between 1890
and 1945, evolved from an overwhelmingly rural, static, and
economically "backward" society to one which approximated the
rest of the nation in important respects. In the first half of the
twentieth century, for example, the percentage of the farm population of the region declined from 58 percent to less than 25 percent. During the same years, the number of industrial workers
increased 500 percent. The plantation agriculture that Roger L.
Ransom and Richard Sutch have recently described had been
bypassed by agricultural technology, industrial growth, and
urban development. The "modern" South was particularly evi-

dent in the developing urban centers of the region. As early as
1920, there were southern cities with dynamic economies and
growing populations—Atlanta, Memphis, Birmingham, Nashville,
Houston, Dallas, and Miami, to mention only a few. By 1950, 60
percent of the region's population lived in what the United
States Census Bureau called "Standard Metropolitan Statistical
Areas."[32]

And yet complete social and political segregation, sanctioned
by custom and enforced by law, existed almost without exception. In the entire history of southern politics from 1890 to 1945,
there were only two possible exceptions to the norm of total
white supremacy in the states of the Old Confederacy. In Memphis, Tennessee, and San Antonio, Texas, black urban dwellers
voted in the thousands at the very nadir of black participation
in southern politics. However limited their impact in the total
context of the region, the very fact of large-scale black political
activism offers a different perspective—and some insight—into
the reasons southern political race relations remained so un-
changing in a half century of economic and demographic transformation.

Of the two cities, the experience of Memphis is perhaps the
best known. Blacks had made up nearly half the voters in that
west Tennessee city in the 1880s and their political influence was
reflected in the election of three black city commissioners and
the appointment of blacks to numerous minor patronage positions. Disfranchisement was as complete in Memphis as the rest
of the South after 1890, but the pattern of substantive black political involvement was renewed within less than fifteen years.
In 1902, Memphis blacks returned to politics on the coattails of
an incumbent mayor, John T. Walsh, who sought unsuccessfully
to hold off a challenge by an independent urban reform movement. While Walsh failed in his bid to remain in office, a young
reform politician named E. H. Crump followed the lead of
Walsh seven years later. Crump had ridden into office as mayor

on a campaign of efficiency and urban reform, but his most significant contribution to southern politics was the utilization of big-city organizational techniques common to northern cities, but relatively undeveloped in the South. With the careful supervision of the police department and the financial support of local saloon owners and friendly businessmen, Crump embraced the techniques of race and ethnic voting. Two years after his election, Crump's organization registered eight thousand blacks—nearly a fifth of the registered voters—and shepherded them to the polls. But the real measure of Crump's skills came in the election of 1914 when complex circumstances led the Memphis boss to undertake one of the most ambitious—if limited—campaigns in black adult education. Forced to wage a write-in campaign to name his handpicked successor, Crump's machine unveiled a sophisticated program of billboards, soundtrucks, and saloon-based classrooms which taught many illiterate Memphis blacks (and whites) to painfully spell out the name of Edward Reichman.[33]

The *Commercial Appeal* echoed the sentiments of many respectable Memphis whites when it recoiled at the "disgusting spectacle" of the Crump machine "conducting schools on Beale Street and seeking to teach gin-drinking niggers enough to mark and write down a name." But Crump succeeded, and for the next twenty years the South witnessed an anomalous situation in which a handful of black leaders bartered their community votes for limited recognition and favors from Boss Crump.[34]

The key black figure in this extraordinary setting was Robert Church, a Yale-educated black Memphis businessman who had grown up in a "brown mansion with crystal chandeliers and mahogany mantels." His father, a self-taught riverboat steward, had built his fortune in the saloons and gambling houses of the river town in the 1870s and 1880s. Despite his impoverished background, Bob Church, Sr. had married well (his wife was a graduate of Oberlin) and prospered. In 1901, Church—like any respectable white businessman—donated $1,000 to underwrite the fortieth reunion of Confederate veterans in Tennessee. Above all else, he saw to it that his son inherited a more respectable position as president of the all-black Solvent Savings and Loan Association of Memphis.[35]

Although Church devoted much of his energy to protecting his position within the Republican party against attacks from the lily white factions, he was the key figure in negotiations between Crump and the black community. Skillfully shifting support from one candidate to another, Church first opposed Crump in elections in 1923 and 1925. Then, in 1927, operating through the "West Tennessee Civic and Political League," he undertook one of the most impressive feats in political organization in the urban South. In a ninety-day period, Church organized the registration of seven thousand additional black voters even though it meant the payment of a two-dollar poll tax at a time when this was a severe economic hardship. In return for the black vote, Crump's handpicked candidate for mayor secretly agreed to pave and light black sections of Memphis, expand facilities for blacks in the city hospital, open additional parks and playgrounds, modify the gross disparity in educational expenditures, and hire black policemen and firemen. Despite a violent and racist campaign led by the two Memphis newspapers, Church's black voters furnished the margin of victory, as blacks went to the polls and voted 20 to 1 in many wards for the Crump candidate.[36]

For blacks, the results of this arrangement were not insignificant. City expenditures in the black community increased substantially (though they were far from equalized); sewers, water service, and city lights were extended into areas almost untouched before the late 1920s. By 1937 three-fourths of the wards in the city's John Gaston Hospital were set aside for blacks, two libraries had been established for the black community, schools and parks were expanded, and black residents of Memphis had obtained well more than half of the federal housing established under New Deal programs. It was, in the words of one black Memphis political leader, the home of the "New South . . . a white South that realizes it cannot rise to its highest and best upon the bleeding breast of a persecuted people."[37]

San Antonio black voters, like those in Memphis, had exercised some political power in the Reconstruction era when blacks had comprised nearly 25 percent of the population and had combined with an independent-minded German minority to give the Republican party a decided majority. Even though San Antonio was in important respects a frontier western community in the late nineteenth century, the presence of a large black population and the liveliness of the racial issues of Reconstruction made it a "southern" city in many ways. Black voting seems to have declined in the latter part of the nineteenth century as the black proportion of the population dwindled to less than 15 percent and the statewide reaction against Negro suffrage affected every area of Texas.[38]

But, in a remarkable turnabout, San Antonio blacks regained the franchise in the years from 1910 to 1940. Despite the existence of an explicit state law prohibiting black voting in the Democratic primary, San Antonio blacks voted in large numbers in the state's Democratic primaries after 1910 and played a key role in San Antonio's politics for the next three decades. Here, too, there was a convergence of interests between a powerful urban political machine and a black electorate anxious to exercise the franchise.

A little-known Texas politician named John Tobin was the originator of this unlikely episode in Texas politics. As sheriff of Bexar County from 1900 to 1912, he was a key figure in the Callahan machine that had dominated the city of San Antonio and surrounding Bexar County for two generations. According to local folklore, Tobin had called upon the citizenry to join a posse in 1910 to track down a well-known desperado. When only blacks volunteered, Tobin hesitated, then swore them in as a *posse comitatus*. The warm gratitude that these black Texans expressed to Tobin supposedly gave him the inspiration for urging the Callahan machine to encourage black voter registration. Blacks, who made up nearly 10 percent of the population, would be docile and properly appreciative for limited favors. And they would certainly be an asset to a political machine increasingly vulnerable to the complaints of middle-class urban reformers.[39]

The exact reasons for Tobin's decision are clouded and uncertain. Perhaps he simply had the same kind of cynical realism that his brother, the fire chief of San Antonio, had exhibited when he sent the local doughboys off to World War I with the admonition that it was "better to be a live son-of-a-bitch than a dead hero."[40] In any case, when Tobin became mayor of San Antonio in 1918 and assumed control of the old Callahan machine he institutionalized the practice of voting blacks in the primaries as well as in the general election. With princely disdain he ignored the angry efforts of the state Democratic party to exclude blacks from the primaries of Bexar County. And he carefully groomed a special black assistant, Charlie Bellinger.[41]

Charlie Bellinger was not cut from the same mold as Robert Church, Jr. of Memphis. Young Bob Church's fortune had been cleansed by a generation of respectable investments, while Bellinger made little attempt to conceal his illicit sources of income. Initially protected by his mentor, John Tobin, Bellinger settled into the black community of San Antonio with a well-protected numbers racket which ultimately employed dozens of runners and subsidiary employees. During the 1920s he had expanded his financial empire into bootleg whiskey. When prohibition ended, he was ready to move into the saloon business without a hitch. Increasingly independent of the old Callahan organization, Bellinger built a well-oiled black machine which turned out five thousand to eight thousand voters—60 percent of those blacks eligible to vote in the city. Even though blacks made up less than 10 percent of the population, they normally cast more than 25 percent of all the votes in San Antonio. Charlie Bellinger's tight control of the black vote gave him a leverage greater than any other black political figure in the early twentieth-century South.[42]

Something of Bellinger's power could be seen in 1935. The previous year, he had been fined thirty thousand dollars and sent up to Leavenworth for an eighteen-month vacation for shortchanging Uncle Sam. The fine was no problem—a few weeks' receipts from the outposts of Bellinger's numbers empire —but the accommodations at Leavenworth were something else again. Through a few close associates, Bellinger informed his white Texas allies that—unless he was promptly released before the 1936 election—he would not answer for the consequences. This warning sent some of the most prominent southwest Texas Democrats to their desks composing letters to President Roosevelt which extolled the sterling character of this, one of Texas's "finest colored citizens." While his friends managed to engineer a parole in early 1936, Bellinger let it be known that nothing short of a full and unconditional pardon would be satisfactory. That demand sent San Antonio's mayor, Charles Quinn, scurrying to Washington in a desperate attempt to intervene directly with President Roosevelt on Bellinger's behalf. Fortunately for San Antonio's white politicos, Bellinger's sudden death in 1936 relieved them of the embarrassment of further supplications on behalf of their black ally.[43]

As in Memphis, such political muscle was not without benefits to the black community. In contrast to the Chicano ghettoes of San Antonio, black neighborhoods had paved streets, equal teachers' salaries in the schools, and a range of city services which compared favorably with any other city in the South. Bellinger's son Velmo was no replacement for his father, and a Harvard education hardly prepared him for the twists and turns of urban politics. Nevertheless, as late as 1941, the old Bellinger machine played a key role in ousting reform mayor Maury Maverick and returning their good friend former mayor Quinn to office.[44]

The rather remarkable careers of the Bellingers of San Antonio and the Churches are almost unique in southern politics in the years from 1890 to 1945. The exact reasons for their limited success still await a satisfactory analysis, but they seem to be linked to a series of unusual circumstances. In both cities traditional white southern leadership groups had been disrupted. In Memphis the great yellow fever epidemics of the 1880s had created a discontinuity among white elites which made possible the rise of alternative leadership groups. In San Antonio, the transient leadership of the huge military base in that city created a leadership vacuum. A perceptive observer of twentieth-century San Antonio observed a similar absence of community political involvement by traditional elites. The powerful cattle families had residences in the city, but their ranches (and their main economic interests) were in the Pecos in west Texas. Army officers raised their children in San Antonio, but, as temporary residents, they had little to do with civic affairs. And, for some reason, the rich oilmen of the city never became involved in urban affairs. Their allegiance, and their attention, was focused upon the oil-rich areas around Midland and Corpus Christi.[45]

Thus, both cities were ripe for the emergence of tight-knit political machines with a life of their own, political machines whose well-being and interests occasionally overshadowed the more parochial racial concerns of the larger community. In this respect, the tradition of ethnic participation—the Irish in Memphis and the Irish and Germans in San Antonio—may have established the patterns of bloc political participation more common in the North than in the South.

Such an unusual congruence of circumstances was hardly

typical of most urban areas of the South. In fact, a survey of the major cities of the South with large black populations reflects the extent to which the experiences of Memphis and San Antonio were anomalies. Atlanta and New Orleans, for example, were (by southern standards) large and cosmopolitan cities with sophisticated political traditions. Blacks made up large proportions of the population in both cities (35 percent in Atlanta and 30 percent in New Orleans in 1940). New Orleans had a tradition of "bloc" politics with group participation by Italians, Germans, and Irish and in the Choctaw machine. Blacks had actively participated in electoral politics in the 1870s and 1880s and 1890s. Atlanta's politics were more rigidly controlled by a business elite, but it was a "progressive" group which accepted—even if it did not welcome—change. And the presence of a large black intellectual leadership centered around Atlanta University and a substantial black bourgeoisie formed the basis for a black urban middle class unequaled in size, collective intelligence, and economic power in the South.[46]

Lesser opportunities for political expression existed in other cities where peculiar combinations of white disinterest and black community made possible limited political participation. In Durham, North Carolina, the presence of the largest black corporation in the world—the North Carolina Mutual Life Insurance Company—and the peculiar personal relationship that its founder, Asa Spalding, had established with Durham's white business and political leadership made possible a limited black political involvement in local issues.[47]

Nevertheless, there is no evidence of any substantial black political participation in the border or Deep South states in the years 1890–1945. The experiences of San Antonio and Memphis were anomalies that only highlight the intractable nature of southern politics. Limited political participation would gradually come to a handful of urban areas in the postwar South, but it would take more than two decades of concerted national pressure and a social upheaval before the basic structure of the politics of the twentieth-century South would change.

Like the career of Huey Long, the peculiar racial histories of San Antonio and Memphis are *sui generis*. However much the social and economic relationships of southern society changed between 1890 and 1945, the structure of political race relations remained unshaken. Nevertheless, the story of white southerners' unswerving commitment to maintaining social and political white supremacy is instructive, for it is a sobering reminder that deeply held beliefs are not necessarily altered by the changes that can be measured in the statistics of the economist and the social scientist. The bungalows of suburbia had reshaped the face of the twentieth-century South, but the ghosts who walked their halls at night were refugees from the decaying Georgian mansions of an earlier time.

The Black Southerner's Response to the Southern System of Race Relations: 1900 to Post–World War II

AL-TONY GILMORE

Although historians have frequently quarreled about the origins, growth, and development of the system of race relations in this nation known as segregation, there can be little disagreement with the view that by the turn of the twentieth century segregation had become as much a part of southern civilization as mint juleps, magnolias, and statues in commemoration of those who bore arms for the Confederacy. This system, which received legal sanctioning in the *Plessy* v. *Ferguson* decision of 1896, demanded the separation of the races in the use of all public accommodations and virtually governed the lives of both blacks and whites from cradle to grave. C. Vann Woodward in describing the impact of segregation on the South has written that "up and down the avenues and byways of Southern life appeared with increasing profusion the little sign: 'White Only' or 'Colored.'" Many of these regulations, he continued, "appeared without requirement by law over entrances and exits, at theaters and boarding houses, toilets and water fountains, waiting rooms and ticket windows."[1] In the bulk of instances, blacks suffered most from these Jim Crow arrangements as segregated facilities consistently proved to be unequal facilities. Equally devastating counterparts of the southern race system were disfranchisement, the proliferation of white supremacy doctrines, unprecendented outbreaks of physical violence inflicted upon blacks, and gross unevenness in the administration of justice.

Removed from slavery by less than half a century, black southerners more than any other group were forced to cope with the short end of segregation. Alternatives were few as the major political parties turned deaf ears to blacks locked in the system, and southern disfranchisement ruled out any realistic attempts for political progress. In fact, the mood of the nation was decidedly antiblack as there prevailed a consensus of public opinion—North and, of course, South—that black people were members of an inferior race. Thus, the march of white supremacy mandating white rule and black subordination found itself galloping in full stride when W. E. B. Du Bois wrote in 1903 that "the problem of the twentieth century is the problem of the color-line."[2]

Black southerners, to be sure, were never monolithic in developing strategies for dealing with the system. And regardless of what a black southerner's station in life may have been, they were *all* forced to respond to the system. Historiographically, nonetheless, far too much emphasis has been placed on the alternatives and solutions presented by the black articulate and major black leaders at the expense of developing a framework to include the wide range of alternatives and solutions offered by the black inarticulate, minor black leaders, and black nonleaders.

This is not to suggest that the articulate black response to segregation was not an important one. Rather the attempt of this essay is to widen the picture of those blacks who responded to the system of segregation by including a discussion of both the articulate and the common man.

Quite obviously, common black southerners in the early twentieth century were the direct descendants of Afro-American slaves. Forced to cope with the harsh and bitter realities of the real world, black southerners, much like their forebears, created another world within the white defined world complete with a semi-separate value system, culture, and world view. Relatively unblemished by white standards of logic, ethics, and morality, they developed and nurtured a sense of moral supremacy to counter white supremacy and a unique concept of manhood and womanhood as a defense against blatant racism and oppression. Historians, constantly plagued by a blind faith and overwhelming dependence on the "crutch of print" and related archival materials, have traditionally overlooked or underestimated the value of nonprint materials in exploring the lives of black people who seldom if ever expressed their attitudes, feelings, and emotions in print. But through an examination of their spoken words, songs, sermons, tales, and folklore in general— much of which was committed to memory and passed on from one generation to another—a window is provided through which can be seen the special problems that segregation thrust upon average black southerners and the nature and variety of their responses to those problems. To be sure, the ultilization of folklore as an instrument to gauge and analyze black responses to the southern system is based on the assumption that much of the internal dynamics of the world of average black southerners were, in many ways, a response to the pressures brought on by the dominant and aggressively hostile world of white southerners.

Because the white southern world rarely if ever afforded common blacks an opportunity to dominate or control anything in the larger society, blacks employed the mechanism of folklore —a device by which they could escape the white-dominated world of reality for a fantasy world, saturated with their values and heavily laden with their dreams, in which they were the dominant individuals. Although the world of folklore was, in large part, a world of make-believe, many of the stories and tales were well grounded in actual incidents that in time grew into the stuff of which legends are made. As C. Eric Lincoln has written: "Every black community in the South has its multitudes of legends illustrating blacks' superior strength, sexual prowess and moral integrity. 'Mr. Charlie' is never a match for the cunning of 'Ol' John.' And 'Miss Ann,' though she is 'as good a ol' white woman' as can be found anywhere, remains in the minds of the black southerner a white woman, and therefore, a legitimate target for the machinations of her black servant, 'Annie Mae.' "[3]

The actual worth of folklore in the lives of black southerners can best be appreciated through an analysis of its themes and the relationship of those themes to reality. In the real world whites dominated by sheer force, power, and brute strength over the powerless and economically dependent southern blacks. In folklore, this world was turned upside-down as the weak triumphed over the strong through wit, ingenuity, guile, and cunning. One story that demonstrates this point concerns a white revenue agent during prohibition who was out trying to catch Sam, a black bootlegger. The revenue agent's trick was to coax Sam into revealing the source of his illegitimate spirits. "Say boy," the agent called to Sam, "come here." Sam responded to the call and approached the revenue agent who flashed a ten-dollar bill. "I'll give you this if you get me a quart of whiskey," said the agent. Sam smiled and said, "Yessir but a quart of whiskey will cost you forty dollars." Determined to make an arrest, the agent agreed and gave Sam forty dollars. Sam accepted the money and asked the agent, "Will you hold this shoe box until I go around the corner to get the whiskey?" The agent agreed and Sam left but after one hour had not returned from around the corner. By that time, the agent decided to look into the shoe box only to find one quart of whiskey with a price tag which read: "ten dollars on some days and forty dollars on others."[4]

Again, in the real southern world white men consistently took sexual advantage of black women while strongly forbidding any sexual contact between black men and white women, even to the point of lynching and castrating black men accused of intimate associations with white women. In black folklore, the coin was cleverly turned as the theme of black men possessed with genital superiority and performing sexual acts with white women became standard. As a result of the frequency and vividness of that theme and the fact that the crudeness and obscenity of the stories were never intended for the printed word, an example of folklore to drive this point home is not considered necessary as this historian succumbs to the difficulty of being accurate and precise without being overly descriptive.

One very important function of folklore in the defensive repertoire of black southerners was its ability to afford an opportunity to laugh at a world that in any rational sense called for tears and anger and not smiles and humor. As Lawrence Levine shows in his recent study *Black Culture and Black Consciousness,* black laughter "was one of the mechanisms Negroes in the United States devised not only to understand the situations they faced but also to mute their effect, to release suppressed feelings, to minimize suffering, [and] to assert the invincibility of their own persona."[5] Most jokes and stories dealing with race relations were particularly humorous when Jim Crow was shown to "backfire" on the white southerners. One story of this type describes the efforts of a black man to purchase a car in Atlanta. The white salesman greets him, but constantly refers to him as "boy." The black man chooses a car and says he wishes to wait a day for a final decision. On the next day, he returns and is greeted by the salesman with "Glad to see you, boy. You'll be proud of this car; not another boy in Atlanta will have a better one." "Sorry," the black man replies, "but the deal is off. I read the law last night and it says minors cannot purchase cars in Georgia and since I am a boy as you have so frequently reminded me, it would be illegal to buy a car from you."[6]

The humor and concealed malice in the Jim Crow stories indicate widespread contempt for the poll tax, sharecropping, segregated schools, southern politicians, southern "crackers," segregated facilities and the myriad of injustices resulting from the system. Still, the ability to make light of such dire situations through displays of black wit in the face of Jim Crow adversities enabled blacks to demonstrate the absurdity of the logic of Jim Crowism and their absolute refusal to see that logic as anything other than a joke.

One story on the literacy test for voting indicates well that blacks understood what it meant. It involves a black foreign language professor who wants to vote in the southern town where his college is located. To vote he must pass the test and is given a newspaper and asked what it says. He reads from it and also reads Spanish, French, and German papers in succession. Then he is given a Chinese paper and triumphantly asked what it says. Unable to read Chinese, he throws it down saying, "It says Negroes can't vote in this town!"[7]

Benjamin Davis, black southern political activist, understood as did most blacks the reality of the southern system when he spoke of his home state. "The Negroes knew very well," said Davis, "that the U.S. Constitution had no bearing in Georgia. They knew that the law was what the 'white folks' said it was."[8] But life was still something to be lived in the fullest, because the land of Jim Crow was also the land of the family, friends, romances, music, religion, chittlin' struts, fish fries, and barbecues. And in the context of all this, blacks relentlessly joked, jibed, questioned, and vigorously rejected the unethical, immoral, illogical, and crude character of the system. Their life and protest became one and the same as their walk, talk, music, tales, styles, and particularly heroes frequently became symbols of protest and resistance to a "dominant" white value system that negated the basic worth of blacks as human beings.

There is much to be learned about any nation, country, or group of people through an analysis of the heroes of those nations, countries, or groups of people. Just as the elevation of Davy Crockett, Charlie Chaplin, and Charles Lindbergh to the level of hero status casts light on how Americans at various times have perceived the essence of themselves, an examination of the heroes of black southerners yields similar results. Strongly admired personality types were those who boldly contested the outer boundaries of expected behavior. The wide oral currency of the exploits of such heroes may be used as documents for gauging black social attitudes. Jack Johnson, the black boxing champion, for example, was popular to the black masses not only because he symbolized what blacks could do when given the opportunity to compete with whites on an equal basis, or because his physical skills discredited notions of white supremacy, but also because of a publicized lifestyle replete with romantic affairs with white women coupled with an adamant refusal to acknowledge racist laws, customs, and traditions.[9] For such a hero, a folklore developed that cuts thin the line between fact and fiction with the admiration remaining constant. The following folklore is offered as an example:

Jack Johnson went to a Jim Crow hotel and asked the desk clerk for a room. When the clerk raised and saw that the man was black, he angrily responded, "We don't serve your kind here." Johnson again asked for a room and the clerk replied the same. The champion then laughed, pulled out a roll of money and politely told the clerk, "Oh you misunderstand me, I don't want it for myself, I want it for my wife—she's your kind."[10]

During the 1930s, boxing champion Joe Louis was also a powerful hero to black southerners, as novelist Ernest Gaines understood when he spoke in the words of a black southerner, Miss Jane Pittman:

Like in the depression, Joe Louis was for the colored. When times got really hard, really tough, He always send you somebody. In the Depression it was tough on everybody but twice as hard on the colored, and He sent us Joe. Joe was a lift to the colored people's heart. Of course, S'mellin' beat him the first time. But that was just to teach us a lesson. . . . And to show us we could take just a little bit more hardship than we thought we could take at first.[11]

Likewise, Maya Angelou captured the meaning of a Louis bout to black southerners in her autobiography *I Know Why The Caged Bird Sings*. The black farmers and workers in and around Stamps, Arkansas, would gather in her grandmother's general store around the store radio seated in rows of chairs, stools, and upturned wooden boxes that had been set up for the occasion. Some stood tightly packed against the walls of the store while children overflowed outside. When Louis appeared to be in trouble all noise and movement ceased. It was not just one black man against the ropes, it was our people falling. It was another lynching, yet another black man hanging on a tree. One more woman ambushed and raped. A black boy whipped and maimed. It was hounds on the trail of a man running through slimy swamps. It was a white woman slapping her maid for being forgetful. We didn't breathe. We didn't hope. We waited. And when Louis, as usual, would rally to win, pandemonium would break loose throughout the general store. "It would take an hour or more before the people would leave the store and head for home. Those who lived too far had made arrangements to stay in town. It wouldn't do for a black man and his family to be caught on a lonely country road on a night when Joe Louis had proved that we were the strongest people in the world."[12]

The arrogant and irrepressible personality of blues singer Huddie Lead Belly made him widely admired as a black rebel throughout the black South. The following "Leadbelly" story is one that has countless variations, but offers a glimpse at understanding why he had such a strong identification with black southerners:

All da women loved him an' followed him round listenin' to da
guitar. We all loved him. I loved him too till I heard he cut
people up. He had a mean streak. He come to town an' was
walkin' down the street an' Dick Ellett called him a "nigger"
an tried to run him off the street, tellin' him not to come back
wid his guitar. An' he pulled out his knife an' cut Dick Ellett
all up. You know, he wouldn't take nothin'. He wouldn't let
nobody push him around.[13]

Aside from those who achieved hero status on the national
level, scores upon scores of blacks at the local level were greatly
admired by black southerners for various exploits of challenging
the system. These hard heroes or "bad niggers" were highly,
though oftimes surreptitiously, worshipped for refusing to accept
the white world's definition of their place in society or the white
dictates on the manner in which they should live. One vital function served by these heroes was the vicarious experience they
gave common blacks, if only for a fleeting moment, of leaving
their demeaning positions. In many ways these heroes became
the flesh and blood embodiments of black folklore figures such
as Shine, Staggolee, Petey Wheatstraw, John Henry, and others
whose notoriety rests on displays of strength, wit, boldness, and
courage in the face of adversity.[14]

Gunnar Myrdal, author of *The American Dilemma,* indicated
little appreciation of folklore as a mechanism for understanding
the average black man when he commented that they "do not
spend too much of their mental energy theorizing over the Negro
problem. Their days are filled with toil and more personal troubles and pleasures."[15] Had Myrdal and others understood that a
unique value system operated beneath this veil of complacency
with the "problem," the result would have been an enlarging of
the operational definition of accommodation. For just as slaves
resisted slavery on a day to day basis through the destruction of
property, feigning of illnesses, running away, work slow-downs,
and general deception, black southerners—though exceptionally

vulnerable to economic reprisals, physical threats, and violence—
resisted the system through the sustaining of a value system
whose roots ran deep into the slavery experience, and perhaps
nowhere was that value system held so firmly intact as it was in
folklore.

Aside from the average black southerner's response to the system as expressed in Afro-American folklore, black southerners
both inarticulate and articulate offered a number of more tan-
gible alternatives for dealing with the system. Such alternatives
included violence, accommodation, the creating and sustaining
of black businesses and institutions, radical political involvement,
migration and emigration schemes, and the development and
continuation of a protest movement complete with a protest
ideology. All such alternatives, however, have interesting counterparts in the folklore.

Violence

When H. Rap Brown, former chairman of the Student Non-
Violent Coordinating Committee, widened the theme of John
Hope Franklin's *The Militant South* in his statement that "violence is as American as cherry pie," he might have added that
violence between blacks and whites in the twentieth-century
South is as southern as fried chicken and watermelon. For
southern whites, the committment to the use of force to maintain
the southern system was as frequent and determined as mani-
festations of discontent and insubordination towards the system
on the part of black southerners. Normally, such physical atrocities against blacks as lynchings, beatings, and whippings were
more likely to cause black retaliation in the form of violence than
disfranchisment or Jim Crow regulations. Yet it was the totality
of the pressure brought on by the system that created an environ-
ment highly susceptible to frequent outbursts of violence from
black southerners.

Some black leaders understood the necessity of individual and collective use of violence in instances of self-defense. Between the years 1905 and 1935, W. E. B. Du Bois approved the use of violence in self-defense and even went so far as to predict a war between the races. James Weldon Johnson also supported violence in self-defense as he felt "the resort to force remains and will doubtless remain the rightful recourse of oppressed peoples."[16] But as Arnold H. Taylor has so perceptively written: "In advocating physical resistance to attack, black leaders were endorsing a principle that the black masses were already practicing."[17] In Georgetown, South Carolina, in 1900 a crowd numbering close to a thousand blacks armed with weapons surrounded a jail to prevent an expected attempt by whites to lynch a black man who had killed a white law officer in an argument over taxes. In New Orleans in 1900, Robert Charles, a black man, shot a white policeman in self-defense and before being killed took refuge in a house and held off a mob of more than a thousand whites, killing seven and wounding nine others in the process. This single act of defiance, which caused the New Orleans race riot, propelled Charles to immediate hero status among the masses of blacks, and for years to come, "the Robert Charles song" was often played at all-black gatherings.[18] Other outbreaks of violence such as the Brownsville, Texas, affair of 1906, the Atlanta riot of 1906, the Jack Johnson riots of 1910, and the riots of 1919 in Elaine, Arkansas, Houston, and Longview, Texas indicate the extent of black retaliation to the southern system in the form of violence.

Individual acts of violence against blacks by whites received considerably less attention than those conflicts involving large numbers, but were far more typical. For example, H. C. Bearley of Clemson College through an examination of the *Columbia State* newspaper from 1925 to 1928 found accounts of 89 interracial homicides in South Carolina, including 57 blacks killed by whites and 32 whites killed by blacks. Of these homicides 23 blacks were killed by white law enforcement officers and 5 officers slain by blacks.[19] The implications of Bearley's study for the entire South and for a longer period of time make clear the widespread atmosphere of violence between black and white southerners.

Accommodationists

Given the power and influence of the southern system to enforce its laws, customs, and way of life and the fact that black southerners understood the force of that power and influence, most black southerners to some extent accommodated the system. The more important issue is the extent to which various blacks were willing to accept the rules of the system and the philosophies nurtured to rationalize those levels of acceptance. It was not uncommon for many blacks branded as accommodationists and "Uncle Toms" to shed long-worn masks of complacency when opportunity presented itself. One popular story illustrates this point well.

The governor of Mississippi called a convention of all the governors. And he wanted to show them the colored people were treated all right in the South. So he called the old colored man over and said, "Sam, when you're hungry we take care of you, don't we?"

"Yessuh, Boss."

"And when you need a new suit, we give you one, don't we?"

"Yessuh, Boss."

"And if you need some money, we'll put some in your pocket, won't we?"

"Yessuh, Boss."

"All right now Sam, just step up to this mike here and tell all the people how we take care of you."

Sam he goes to the mike, and he says, "Who am I talking to, Boss?"

And the governor says, "You're talking to Washington, D.C., and New York, and the high country up north."

"You mean I'm not talking to Alabama, Georgia, Mississippi?"
"No, Sam."
So Sam hollers into the mike, "HELP! HELP! HELP!"[20]

No single black personality of the twentieth century developed a philosophy of accommodation more palatable to white supporters of the southern system than Booker T. Washington. Washington helped to found Tuskegee Institute in 1881 and persuaded influential white southerners and northern philanthropists that it was in the best interest of the South and the nation to educate blacks in the mechanical, industrial, and agricultural arts. He also pleased whites with his urging of blacks to give up immediate quests for political rights and social equality and to focus instead on advancing themselves economically and morally. A master publicist and astute propagandist, Washington became the most powerful black American from 1895, when he unveiled his philosophy in the famous "Atlanta Exposition Address," until his death in 1915. Working from his base at Tuskegee Institute, where he served as principal, his school of thought and those who supported it became known as the "Tuskegee Machine." Much has been written about that organization and Booker T. Washington, but no scholar to date has been able to assess with accuracy the extent of acceptance of his total program among the masses of black southerners.[21]

To black southerners who understood the intensity of white opposition to political and social equality, and who believed that economic advancement could *upgrade the quality of the inequality* resulting from the system, Washington's philosophy must have sounded reasonable and practical. To sound reasonable and practical, of course, does not usually result in the conversion of disciples to a particular point of view. Nevertheless, the scarcity of workable alternatives to the system forced many blacks to condone, if not completely accept, Washington's plan. Interestingly, in recent years scholars have uncovered documents which reveal that Booker T. Washington did not always practice what he preached and often worked surreptitiously behind the image of his philosophy to support protest efforts.

In capsule, Washington believed that his philosophy would produce a core of black businessmen, farmers, and artisans for the agricultural and industrial fields. This vanguard of black workers, he reasoned, would gain the respect of white southerners who, out of a sense of economic justice and fair play, would accord blacks their political rights. Washington's single greatest weakness was his inability to speak out on the vital relationship between political rights and economic advancement. And because of this pivotal blunder, oversight, or strategic concession, his long-range objectives were destined to failure.

After Booker T. Washington's death his philosophy was continued by a crop of post-1915 Bookerites led by Robert Russa Moton, the new principal of Tuskegee. However, none of this group was able to promote the accommodationist philosophy as successfully as had Washington.

Creating and Sustaining Black Businesses and Institutions
In a sense the segregation or Jim Crow laws and customs of the southern system gave rise to a class of southern black businessmen who actually profited economically by providing blacks with goods and services denied by white businesses. Most of these businesses catered to black clientele only and were generally inferior to their white counterparts in efficiency, variety of stock, resources, expertise, appearance, and location. The most successful of these businesses were undertaking establishments, restaurants, beauty and barber shops, motor transportation and entertainment facilities.

One of the more outstanding achievements of a black business in the Jim Crow South was the phenomenal growth and development of the North Carolina Mutual Life Insurance Company of

Durham, North Carolina, which ranked as the nation's foremost black business throughout the Jim Crow era. The founders of this company—John Merrick, A. M. Moore, and C. C. Spaulding —were all dedicated disciples of the accommodationist philosophy expounded by Booker T. Washington. Understanding the sensitive nature of politics and race relations in the South, this triumvirate accommodated the system on questions of social and political equality and set an example for all on the potential of the black economy.[22]

A number of black southerners of integrationist persuasion also came to view the black economy as a source of potential economic and political power and recognized the concomitant value of black businesses. This view is well expressed in folklore:

This colored man had worked up a nice trade selling ice in a community. And all the people in that community, both white and colored, was buying from him. The white man began selling ice too, since the colored man was doing so well he thought he would go in there and get him some customers.

So when the white woman saw the colored woman had changed to the white man—the white woman was still buying from the colored man—she said, "Now why did you stop buying from John, he was so courteous and nice, and we did business with him a long time?"

"Well I tell you truth Miz George, I tell you just why I changed—that white man's ice is just colder than that nigger's ice."

(They told that tale to try to get colored people to patronize each other, when their things were just as good as the white man's.)[23]

By the mid-1930s W. E. B. Du Bois had come to reconsider the role of segregation as a tool for integration and called for blacks to buy at black stores, patronize black professional men, to amuse themselves at black resorts and theaters, and to support black enterprises in general. Only after establishing a solid economic base, he reasoned, would measurable progress towards integration be made. Marcus Garvey had come to this conclusion about segregation and black business in the 1920s, although he eschewed integration as an ultimate objective. Black southerners came out in large numbers to hear Garvey speak on his tours throughout the South, and most accounts of those trips indicate that he was favorably received.[24]

The response of black southerners to the denial of educational opportunity in white educational institutions was simple: build and sustain black ones. Though inadequately funded and drastically short of proper resources, black educational institutions of all levels educated the overwhelming majority of black Americans during the segregation era. Under the doctrine of separate but equal, blacks argued for and received financial support from the southern states. Private black schools also functioned in the South independent of state funds. At all ranks of southern society, blacks understood the unfairness in educational appropriations for black schools. Though quite a bitter pill to swallow, they often dressed the issue in humor and sarcasm. The following folklore is offered: "The appropriation for the Negro school was used for the White school. The superintendent explained this to the Negro principal, who of course couldn't make a direct protest. So he said, 'The one thing we need most of all is educated white folk.' "[25]

During the 1930s black southerners clamored for admission to white educational institutions in the South and challenged the equality of the separate but equal doctrine. With the assistance of the NAACP, important cases were won which admitted blacks to white southern educational institutions. In 1935, Donald Murray was admitted to the University of Maryland Law School. Other cases attempting to admit blacks to white institutions were lost on legal technicalities or displays of outright racism by the courts. Still, the logic of arguing that separate but equal was, de facto, separate and unequal made a formidable case. The admission of Herman Sweat to the University of Texas Law School in 1950 was won because the Supreme Court insisted that the three-room makeshift law school hastily assembled at the black Prairie View College was flagrantly unequal to the law school facilities at the University of Texas. And on May 17, 1954, the Supreme Court broke down the legal barrier of the South's and the nation's segregated school systems when it declared separate schools to be inherently unequal.[26] The role of the black church as a "release valve" from the system cannot be overestimated. In the black church, blacks found in E. Franklin Frazier's words "a refuge from this hostile white world." Opportunity was provided for leadership roles, social activities flourished, hope was sustained, and frustrations and hostilities were given emotional release.

Radical Political Alternatives

Black southerners during the segregation era found themselves scorned by the major political parties and disfranchised to the point of not having any group political clout at the ballot box. Although heavily courted by radical political movements, black southerners appeared to believe that the major political parties and the American system, with the exception of their position on the race question, were closest to the prospects of attaining the goal of an America with justice and equality for all people. In other words, they sought not to destroy or replace the political system but to reform it; they wanted "a piece of the rock."

Following World War I, the Socialist party sought to attract southern blacks but failed miserably with a breathtaking ignorance of the inner dynamics of the black community. Socialists stressed class consciousness across ethnic lines, while blacks generally disliked poor whites. Socialists called for the overthrowing of capitalism in the face of blacks striving for material prosperity, possessions, and the affluent life. During the early 1930s the Communist party made efforts to draw southerners into its fold. Given the additional hardships the depression placed on blacks, the Communists sought to exploit the fertile soil of black unemployment and discrimination. Concentrating on such southern urban areas as Atlanta, Birmingham, and New Orleans, the Communist party anticipated the development of a working-class protest. Wilson Record points out, "Even some Negroes and whites who under no circumstances would embrace the revolutionary goals of the Party, were not too hesitant to join front organizations whose immediate purpose was raising wages, increasing relief payments, or obtaining better terms under tenancy agreements."[27] Thousands of southern blacks united with southern whites under one such front organization, the Share-croppers' Union, and were met with violent resistance from white vigilantes and law enforcement officials. In time any interracial protest organization in the South would become vulnerable to being labeled Communist front organizations and would be subject to being met with strident opposition by the southern power structure.

The sensitivity of the Roosevelt administration to the plight of black southerners, coupled with white opposition to interracial protests, led to the dissolution of the Sharecroppers' Union and similar organizations. Still, it is significant that a small number of southern blacks led by such black personalities as Hosea Hudson and Angelo Herndon sought the Communist party as an alternative to the southern system. As one scholar has recently shown, the radical movements failed to attract and maintain a sufficient number of black followers because, even though their "radical solutions may have promised long range achievement of such goals, . . . capitalism seemed, to many, to promise it a good deal sooner. Blacks wanted *their* piece of the action, and action in America meant Horatio Alger, participation in mainstream economics, and individual salvation through individual economic mobility."[28]

Migration and Emigration Movements

To a small but significant number of black southerners, the impact of the southern system on their lives and the dismal prospects of effecting meaningful change in that system prompted a consideration of returning to Africa. During the latter part of the nineteenth century—a period which Rayford Logan describes as the nadir for blacks in America—organizations such as the American Colonization Society, the Congo National Emigration Company, and the International Migration Society all transported blacks back to Africa.

Bishop Henry McNeal Turner, a black southerner, was perhaps the most widely known and influential leader of the back-to-Africa campaigns of the late nineteenth and early twentieth centuries. For Turner, emigration to Africa offered not only an escape for persecuted black Americans but a chance to develop and build Africa into a great continent, a continent that would be a proud home for blacks throughout the diaspora. For assistance in his emigration schemes Turner demanded, unsuccessfully, that the federal government provide adequate financial support. Throughout the early twentieth-century South, there were occasional bursts of emigration excitement but not of the magnitude to attract large numbers of blacks. One of Turner's problems was the open resentment to his plans by such leading blacks as Booker T. Washington. "For every negro that is sent to Liberia," spoke Washington against Turner, "a negro baby is born in the cotton belt, so that scheme is a failure. As we came to this country at the urgent solicitation and expense of the white man we would be ungrateful to run away and leave him now."[29]

Faced with strong black and white opposition to his movement, Turner continued to hold emigration conventions in such southern cities as Chattanooga, Birmingham, and Montgomery. Unfortunately, due to dwindling interest and severe financial hardships, by 1910 his movement was defunct.

After Turner, the most successful black emigrationist was Chief Alfred Sam's Akim Trading Company which in 1913 sent over one thousand black southerners to Africa, most of them going to Liberia.[30] The back-to-Africa schemes never took hold on the majority of black southerners, and their failures seem to indicate that black southerners, though clearly of African background, were possessed with a present that was uniquely Afro-American. To put it another way, the Afro-American branches of the African tree had taken on an importance that rivaled the African roots.

The availability of employment opportunities in the North during the first World War and the comparative mildness of racial proscriptions in that region of the country ignited a movement of over a half-million blacks away from the South. In lesser but significant numbers southern blacks continued this trend for the next four decades. That immigration without rival constitutes one of the more dramatic responses of black southerners to the southern system.

Radical Intellectuals

Following the 1903 publication of *The Souls of Black Folk*, W. E. B. Du Bois emerged as the leading spokesman for blacks who strenuously took exception to the accommodationist philosophy. In that collection of essays Du Bois sharply criticized Booker T. Washington and called for blacks to be granted complete status as equal citizens. A New Englander by birth, Du Bois's many years as an Atlanta professor and militant protester qualify him as a southerner responding to the system. Writing and working out of Atlanta until 1910, Du Bois was joined by such black southerners as fellow Atlantan J. Max Barber, editor of the militant and shortlived *Voice Of The Negro*. A number of black southerners were also members of the Niagara Movement, a black protest organization, while others frequently arranged coalitions both within and outside of the South and across racial lines in their efforts to bring equal rights to black Americans. Generally these intellectuals called for an immediate cessation of disfranchisement, segregation, and physical violence inflicted upon blacks. They conceptualized the struggle as one that was as much a white problem as a black problem and geared their arguments to the national rather than strict regional levels. Leading members of this category were Benjamin E. Mays, Ida Wells-Barnett, Mary Church Terrell, and P. B. Young.

Du Bois left the South in 1910 to co-found the NAACP and was a major force in extending its influence into the South. By the end of the first World War, NAACP branches existed in every southern state, boasting a combined southern membership of nearly 19,000 persons. Through the NAACP, black southerners had effected a coalition with liberal whites and northern blacks and by the post–World War II period this organization had won legal decisions that undermined the complete foundation on which the southern system stood.

The post–World War II era brought serious consequences on the southern system of race relations. President Harry Truman appointed a Commission on Higher Education which reported in 1947 that "there will be no fundamental correction of the total condition until segregation legislation is repealed." Truman also appointed a Committee on Civil Rights whose report, *To Secure These Rights,* called for the ending of racial segregation. Going even further, Truman issued in 1948 an executive order that called for an end to segregation in the Armed Services. One distinguished scholar has seen fit to call this period the "Second Reconstruction." Without doubt, the reasons for change were many. Chief among them were the forthright and courageous leadership of Truman, the irony and contradiction that the German Nazi movement posed for America's treatment of its black citizens, the growing liberal element of the Democratic party, and *most importantly* the increased intensity and potential of black protest whose roots ran deep into the black southern experience.

Race and Economy in the South, 1890–1950

ROBERT HIGGS[*]

In the South, economic organization and racial relations have always been intertwined. Under slavery the ideal of the masters, often articulated but never fully realized, was to match the economic division of labor with a corresponding racial division: the whites would attend to the tasks requiring thought, responsibility, and management, while the blacks would perform the manual labor. The antebellum society was never wealthy enough to carry this conception into practice, and most whites necessarily had to work hard physically to earn their living. Nevertheless, the white ideal remained a force in shaping racial relations, and the attenuated form of the racial division of labor that did emerge under slavery persisted long after the emancipation of the slaves.

The traditional southern conception of the racial division of labor, growing from roots in the plantation society, applied best to a static, rural economic organization. This is perhaps one reason why white southerners so often succumbed to nostalgia for the Old Regime; in such a world, the whites could most easily sustain their racial dominance. In the first half of the

[*] I am indebted to Stanley Engerman for alerting me to a serious arithmetical mistake in an earlier draft of this paper.

twentieth century, however, the southern economy was rapidly becoming a modern urban-industrial organization, and a pattern of racial relations based on rural, preindustrial conditions could not remain forever viable. The traditional system of racial relations depended on keeping the blacks ignorant, poor, and immobile, the immobility being at once economic, social, and physical. But southern economic development progressively provided people, both the blacks and the whites, with more education and knowledge, higher incomes and living standards, and greater mobility. Hence, the region's economic development increasingly undermined the foundations of its traditional racial relations. As we all know, the South's traditional system of racial relations was resilient; the whites fought hard to preserve their longstanding position of supremacy. But between 1900 and 1950 the emerging internal contradictions of the southern social system threatened it more and more, and in the 1950s and 1960s it finally collapsed. Of course, the federal government did much to hasten its demise. Still, it is difficult to imagine how the crumbling of the traditional system of southern racial relations that has occurred since World War II could ever have taken place in the absence of the region's economic transformation during the previous half-century.

Southern Economic Development, 1890–1950
For almost three decades after the Civil War, economic recovery proceeded fairly steadily in the South. Then the 1890s ushered in a prolonged period of depression in the cotton market that dragged down farmers and townspeople alike. In an important sense, cotton was still king in the Deep South, while tobacco ruled in the Upper South. As late as the 1890s, the vicissitudes of the South's two great cash crops largely determined whether the region would be prosperous or depressed. One can easily see why the South's susceptibility to the tyrannical rule of the cotton and tobacco markets was so great. Over

85 percent of the population remained rural, and about two-thirds of the labor force depended on agriculture for a livelihood. Manufacturing was growing rapidly but from a small base, and during the nineties it provided employment for less than 6 percent of the labor force. The South contained about 30 percent of the nation's population, some 23 million southerners at the turn of the century. Their rate of natural increase was high, over 20 percent per decade. Yet despite the depressed conditions of the 1890s, only a negligible number of southerners migrated out of the region. (A considerable westward migration within the region did occur, Texas and Oklahoma being the principal attractions.) In brief, the southern economy at the end of the nineteenth century provided small cause for optimism. Still predominantly rural and agricultural, with a large, rapidly growing, and relatively immobile population, its level of income per capita only about half the national average, the southern economy gave little indication of how bright its future would eventually be.[1]

At the turn of the century, the southern economy began a period of prosperity and rapid growth that persisted for two decades. As before, cotton led the way; but increasingly the nonagricultural economy provided an independent impetus for economic progress. Cotton prices, which had averaged only 7 cents a pound during the 1890s, rose substantially: they averaged over 10 cents a pound between 1900 and 1915, then skyrocketed to an unprecedented average of 25 cents a pound during 1916–1920, far outstripping the wartime increase of the general price level.[2] As usual, farm prosperity spilled over onto merchants railroads, bankers, and even school boards, and cotton's golden era brought good times to many people besides farmers. The nonfarm sector of the economy grew rapidly during the early twentieth century. By 1920 well over half of the region's labor force found employment outside agriculture, as manufacturing, trade, transportation, and professional services led the advance.

Concomitantly with the growth of the nonfarm economy, urbanization proceeded faster than ever before. By 1920 one-fourth of all southerners lived in cities. Finally, after 1915, many southerners took advantage of new opportunities to find better employment in the North during the world war, and the rate of out-migration from the South became substantial for the first time; net out-migration equaled over 3 percent of the average southern population during the period 1910–1920. After twenty years of relatively rapid economic growth, southern income per capita had increased from 50 to 60 percent of the national average. In sum, during the first two decades of the twentieth century the southern economy performed more progressively than at any time since the Civil War. Southern people were quickly becoming more urbanized, wealthier, and more mobile; southern industry was growing by leaps and bounds. Small wonder that the long-heralded New South seemed at last to be a reality.

Hard times, however, lay just ahead, and the two decades of the interwar period saw substantially lower rates of growth. During the 1920s the southern economy actually stagnated, and the gains in per capita income (relative to the national average) realized during the previous period had largely dissolved before the onset of the Great Depression. Southern real income per capita, in fact, was lower in 1930 than it had been in 1920. Agricultural difficulties accounted in large part for the economic doldrums of the 1920s; problems in the textile industry compounded these difficulties. This time, however, southerners fled from their home region in large numbers to escape its depressed economy. The rate of out-migration, almost 5 percent of the average population during the 1920s, was higher than ever before; if Texas is excluded from the regional definition, the rate becomes much higher, about 7 percent. Many continued to seek material betterment in the cities. Although manufacturing was sluggish, the service sector expanded to absorb those fleeing from a depressed agricultural economy.

The Great Depression of the 1930s, painful as it was for almost everyone, did not hit the South as hard as it hit the North. The manufacturing of durable goods, which was most vulnerable to the business-cycle bust, occupied relatively few in the South. Cotton and tobacco producers benefited from the New Deal price support programs during the mid-thirties. Southern manufacturing employment stagnated, but rapid expansion of employment in the service sector took up much of the slack. Out-migration continued at a high rate, removing 3 percent of the average population during the 1930s. By 1940 only a third of the labor force remained in agriculture; the cities contained more than a third of the population; and real income per capita had reached new absolute highs and largely regained its previous standing relative to the national average. In sum, though the interwar years witnessed considerable economic adversity in the South, the region's people did not accept hard times as their fate. Seeking to better themselves, they migrated to the cities and beyond the region in a steady stream. Within the South, industrialization continued, and on the eve of the second world war the southern income level had reached a new peak.

World War II brought unprecedented economic progress to the South. In the 1940s, real income per capita increased faster than ever before, leaping more than 70 percent and bringing the South at last within hailing distance of the U.S. average. Prosperity was widespread, but differential opportunities in the nonfarm economy still beckoned, and farming employment continued to shrink. Urban employments flourished, and out-migration drew unprecedented numbers to the North and the West —more than 5 percent of the average population during the 1940s. By 1950 southern real income per capita had reached about seven-tenths of the national average (probably even higher if allowance could be made for the lower price level in the South); more than four-tenths of the population lived in cities; and only about two-tenths of the labor force remained in agriculture. Economic modernization had finally come to the South.

Did Both Races Participate?
In considering the extent to which the two races participated in the economic transformation of the South, one must be careful to distinguish two concepts of relative participation. The first is relative position at a certain time, for example, the relative earnings of black workers in 1900. The second is relative rate of change over time, for example, the rate of increase of black incomes between 1900 and 1950 in comparison with the same measure for whites. On several occasions since the Civil War, the blacks have improved their economic condition more rapidly than the whites while remaining below white levels; that is, the racial gap in economic well-being has been narrowed but not completely eliminated. It is well to remember, also, that the economic position of both races, in absolute terms, improved enormously during the first half of the twentieth century; real personal income per capita increased by some 250 percent in the South.

One must also recognize that the relative economic position of the blacks at any time results from the interacting effects of two forces—current effective discrimination and the legacies of past (perhaps currently defunct) discrimination. Slavery left the black population heavily disadvantaged in the pursuit of material betterment. Landlessness, ignorance, illiteracy, ill health, and inexperience in managing their own affairs plagued the freedmen and hampered their descendants for decades after the emancipation. Even if discrimination had magically disappeared in 1865, generations would have passed before the attainment of complete racial economic equality. Of course, no such magic ever happened, and continuing racial discrimination further slowed the narrowing of the economic gap separating the races.

As a benchmark for our survey, consider the sectoral distribu-

TABLE 1   Sectoral Distribution of Gainfully Occupied Persons
in the South, by Race, 1890

Sector	Percent of 4,003,000 whites	Percent of 2,746,000 blacks
Agriculture, fishing, and mining	59	62
Professional services	4	1
Domestic and personal services	9	28
Trade and transportation	13	4
Manufacturing and mechanical trades	15	5

SOURCE: Calculated from data in U.S. Census Office, *Compendium of the
Eleventh Census: 1890* (Washington, 1897), Pt. III, pp. 440–45.

tion of gainfully occupied persons in 1890 (Table 1). At that
time in the South, just under six-tenths of the whites and just
over six-tenths of the blacks reported a gainful occupation in
agriculture. For those occupied in the nonfarm sector, the occupational distributions differed greatly, according to race: three-
quarters of the blacks performed domestic and personal services,
while only one-fifth of the whites did so, most whites in the
nonfarm sector being involved in trade, transportation, and
manufacturing. In addition, the whites had a proportion four
times greater in the professions. The legacy of slavery stands
out clearly even in these crude data. Thirty-five years after the
Civil War, the blacks could still be found, overwhelmingly,
chopping cotton or scrubbing a floor.

In agriculture, where the majority of both labor forces remained at the turn of the century, the blacks worked mainly at
the lower end of the tenure ladder. Proportionately far more
were wage hands. Of those classified as farm operators, relatively few were owners; relatively far more were tenants. In
1910, the census counted 175,000 black farmers in the South

who owned all the land they cultivated, and another 43,000 part owners; yet even then, almost half a century after the Civil War, 75 percent of the black operators rented all the land they cultivated. White tenants, by contrast, constituted only 40 percent of all white farm operators in the South (Table 2). Once again, the legacy of slavery and the landless emancipation stood out in bold relief.

TABLE 2   Tenure Distribution of Farm Operators in the South, by Race, 1910

Tenure class	Percentage of 2,207,000 white farm operators	Percentage of 890,000 black farm operators
Full owners	52	20
Part owners	8	5
Fixed-rent tenants[a]	10	32
Share-rent tenants[b]	29	43
Managers	1	[c]

[a] Some fixed-rent contracts required the tenant to pay the landlord a prescribed sum of money ("cash rent"), while others required payment of a fixed quantity of products ("standing rent"). The census did not distinguish these forms, employing the expression "cash rent" for both kinds of fixed rent.
[b] Before 1920, the census did not distinguish "sharecroppers" (share tenants to whom the landlord furnished work stock) from other tenants paying share rents.
[c] Less than 1 percent.

SOURCE: Calculated from data in U.S. Bureau of the Census, *Negro Population, 1790–1915* (Washington, 1918), 609, 612.

As the southern economy was transformed after 1900, both the black and the white labor forces underwent similar changes in their occupational distributions. In both cases, relative involvement in agriculture shrank. By 1940, only a third of employed white males and less than half of employed black males worked on farms. (These counts include substantial numbers of unpaid family workers.) In both cases the relative importance of unskilled laborers declined, while the relative number of semiskilled operatives increased. Even more precipitous changes occurred during the 1940s, as agriculture contracted to employ only a fifth of the white males and a third of the black males in the South. Table 3 provides a more detailed description of the

TABLE 3   Occupational Distribution of the Labor Force in the South, by Race and Sex, 1950

	White		Black	
	Male	Female	Male	Female
Major Occupational Group	(percent)	(percent)	(percent)	(percent)
White Collar Occupations	30.9	58.8	5.8	10.6
Professional and technical	6.8	13.3	2.0	6.2
Managers and Proprietors	11.4	5.4	1.4	1.2
Clerical	5.8	29.3	1.6	2.2
Sales	6.9	10.8	0.8	1.0
Blue Collar Occupations	36.7	20.6	24.6	9.6
Craftsmen and foremen	18.3	1.3	6.3	0.3
Operatives	18.4	19.3	18.3	9.3
Unskilled Labor and Service	9.8	13.8	34.3	64.0
Laborers (exc. farm and mine)	5.7	0.5	23.3	1.6
Service (exc. household)	3.5	10.4	10.1	17.7
Private household workers	0.6	29.3	0.9	44.7
Farm Occupations	21.5	3.8	33.8	13.9
Farmers and farm managers	15.5	0.9	19.3	2.5
Farm laborers and foremen	6.0	2.9	14.5	11.4
Occupation not reported	1.3	2.9	1.3	1.7

SOURCE: U.S. Census data cited in Vivian W. Henderson, *The Economic Status of Negroes: In the Nation and In the South* (Atlanta, 1963), 17.

occupational structure, by race and sex, in the South in 1950.

This similarity of the occupational trends for the two races deserves emphasis, because the tendency of social scientists and historians has been to stress cases where blacks lost ground more than cases where they gained. To provide a comprehensive view, one must consider changes in the labor force as a whole. The analysis that comes closest to doing this appears in Gary Becker's *Economics of Discrimination,* where he constructs an index of relative occupational standing for black males employed in the nonagricultural economy of the South. This index falls from 0.67 in 1910 to 0.63 in 1940, then rises to 0.65 in 1950.[3] The index is not sufficiently accurate to measure small changes sensitively. Probably the most warranted inference is that blacks were almost holding their own over time; they were not gaining occupational ground relative to the whites, but neither were they losing much ground. They were steadily upgrading themselves, but the gap between the average white and the average black occupation stayed proportionately about the same during the first half of the twentieth century in the nonagricultural economy of the South. One should also consider, however, that white males were abandoning agriculture slightly faster than blacks. Moreover, Becker's index applies only to males; therefore it does nothing to gauge the relative occupational standing of black females in the South.

Racial similarities are evident when one examines the urbanization of the southern population. In fact, throughout the entire period between 1890 and 1950, during which the southern population went from 13 percent to 42 percent urban, the proportion urban remained almost identical for blacks and whites. Whatever the opportunities in southern cities, both races sought access to them in similar degree.

In out-migration from the South, however, a clear racial difference existed. In every decade the out-migration rate for blacks exceeded that for whites. The rate for whites reached its maximum during the period of World War I, though even then it equaled only half the black rate. The out-migration rate for blacks increased substantially during the 1920s, fell back during the Great Depression, then reached unprecedented peaks during

World War II. For the 1940s, the rate of out-migration was an almost incredible 17 percent of the average population for blacks but only 3 percent for whites. Clearly, the blacks believed they had more to gain in the North and the West.

To what extent did incomes increase for the two races in the South during the first half of the twentieth century? This question cannot be answered with precision, because income data were never systematically and comprehensively compiled by race until 1940, and all income data for this period are more or less unreliable. I have tried to shed light on a part of this statistical darkness by constructing a crude estimate for *circa* 1900. My estimate indicates that black income per capita at the turn of the century probably equaled about 35 percent of the corresponding white level for the entire United States. Some rough checks confirm that this estimate lies in the correct neighborhood, but no one should place great faith in its precision.[4] My estimate, in conjunction with the fact that southern income per capita was 50 percent of the national average, implies that the income per capita of southern blacks was about two-thirds of the southern white level. Estimates by William Vickery indicate that the relative income of southern blacks probably changed little between 1900 and 1940. Vickery's estimates suggest some relative improvement between 1910 and 1920, then relative losses during the 1920s and, especially, during the 1930s. In 1940, when the census first collected such information, southern blacks had annual earnings equal to just under 40 percent of southern white earnings.[5] Relative gains definitely occurred during the 1940s, and at mid-century the average income level of blacks stood at about 45 percent of the corresponding white level.[6]

Both races participated in the economic transformation of the South between 1900 and 1950. While both became urbanized to the same extent, the whites apparently experienced somewhat greater occupational upgrading and income gains. Overall, economic well-being improved for both groups, but the economic position of the blacks relative to the whites probably deteriorated during the interwar period. Over the long run the relative gap was not being closed. In view of this widening racial disparity, the extraordinarily high rates of black out-migration are more easily understood. Evidently, during the first half of the twentieth century in the South, the battle for achievement of racial economic equality had been fought and lost.

Racial Discrimination: Why, Where, How, How Effective?
The gap was not narrowed because racial discrimination continued to withhold from blacks the principal means of narrowing it. That general statement is, however, virtually a truism; without further explication, it conveys no information. Too often the puzzle of racial economic inequality has been solved by pointing to unspecified acts of discrimination. Economists in particular have been guilty of treating discrimination as, in their jargon, a "residual": what remains after objectively measurable differences in productivity characteristics have been considered and found insufficient to account fully for observed racial differences in incomes, earnings, or occupational distributions. To go beyond this primitive mode of analysis, one must consider, at the very least, why the whites wanted to discriminate, where and how they did so, and how effective their discriminatory actions were.

As an economist, I am not especially well qualified to address the issue of why the whites wanted to discriminate against the blacks. Psychologists, sociologists, historians, and other sagacious people have considered this problem at length, and I can add nothing instructive to what they have already said. I raise the issue, nevertheless, because what one assumes about *why* the whites desired to discriminate has implications for the question of *how* they discriminated. Once again to use the economist's language, the way one "models" discrimination for purposes of analysis depends crucially on one's assumptions, perhaps only implicit assumptions, about why the whites wanted to discriminate against the blacks in the first place.

For the past two decades most economists have studied discrimination within the framework of the so-called "neoclassical model" devised by Gary Becker. The specification of that model says nothing explicitly about why the whites want to discriminate, but it is clear from the stated assumptions that the reason is a white aversion to physical contact with blacks. This implicit assumption poorly represents the historical reality of southern white racism. (Whether it applies more accurately to northern white racism I leave as a moot point on this occasion.) Southern society for centuries brought blacks and whites physically together without any repulsion whatever. It is quite misleading, in general, to picture southern whites as disliking blacks individually and as being prepared to pay a price to avoid physical proximity to them. In my judgment, Donald Dewey was correct when he observed that "cases where employers deliberately sacrifice profits in order to indulge an animosity toward Negroes are extremely rare" and further that "individuals acting on their own will pay virtually nothing for the satisfaction of being served by a white clerk."[7]

A more accurate representation of southern white racism is that the whites at large desired to keep the blacks at large subordinate—economically, socially, and in every other way. Such group subordination was perfectly consistent with absolute economic progress by blacks and in no way precluded friendly and even cordial relations between individual members of the two races. It did require, however, what we may call Dewey's First Law: black workers could not hold jobs that required them to give orders or advice to whites. Dewey also propounded a Second Law: blacks and whites could not work side by side at the same jobs. He recognized, however, that the Second Law was commonly violated in "dirty, low-wage, and generally low 'net advantage' employment." In fact, so much of the employment available in the South belonged in this exempted category that the exception probably became the rule; as Dewey himself observed, members of the two races worked side by side throughout the South.[8]

Combining the perspectives opened up by Becker's model with a more realistic assumption about why the whites desired to discriminate, we are led to several testable hypotheses. One is that wage discrimination—where an employer paid blacks less than whites for doing the same work under the same conditions —was uncommon in the South. A second hypothesis is that the black labor force was concentrated either in jobs where blacks did not give orders nor advice or in jobs segregated from whites altogether. A third hypothesis, suggested by Dewey, is that color lines and black earnings moved back and forth as population movements altered the racial composition of the labor market.[9] To assess these hypotheses, we must scrutinize the evidence.

At the turn of the century, the United States Department of Agriculture collected a massive quantity of information on the wages paid to blacks and whites working in southern agriculture. This information shows that, on average, whites received about 8 percent larger money wages than blacks, the difference being that between 80 and 74 cents per day for ordinary labor without board. The department's reports stressed, however, that although whites received higher wages in money, blacks more commonly received rations as a supplement to their money wages; and taking into account the value of the rations, total real wages differed little, if at all, between members of the two races working for wages on farms. This absence of racial wage discrimination is not surprising. Farm employers generally regarded black and white wage labor as perfectly substitutable; and, as a report to the U.S. Industrial Commission observed, "any white labor of the same grade of service is leveled in the competition." In short, with widespread competition for labor in a market containing thousands of employers, few of whom would pay whites a premium for the color of their skin, systematic racial wage differentials could not be sustained.[10]

Recent econometric studies of the agricultural land rental market have reached similar conclusions. In the Georgia cotton belt in 1900, for example, scholars once considered the racial composition of the population as the decisive determinant of prevailing land rental contracts. In fact, however, there was little difference between blacks and whites in a particular county: in the predominantly white areas both black and white tenants tended to obtain share-rent contracts; in the predominantly black areas both black and white tenants tended to obtain fixed-rent contracts. Across counties, the rental mix for blacks and the rental mix for whites were highly correlated ($r = 0.91$). Another recent study found that among the southern states in 1910, variations in the rental mix—the percentage of acreage rented for shares in all acreage rented by full tenants—were significantly associated with variations in yield risk but were not significantly associated with the race of the tenants. Thus, econometric studies have confirmed the judgment of a Georgia planter who told the U.S. Industrial Commission in 1900, "The contracts are made on the same basis to each race." Apparently, competition in the land rental market precluded the emergence of racial differences in contractual forms, other things being the same.[11]

In nonagricultural employments, evidence of racial wage discrimination is easy to find. The problem is that this evidence is fragmentary and insufficient to support reliable generalizations. I know of only one systematic study of racial wage discrimination in southern nonfarm occupations that has analyzed firm-specific data.[12] This study considers 11 occupations for 1900 and 14 occupations for 1909 in Virginia. Its unit of observation is the "contract," which means in this instance the daily wage rates paid by a specific firm to workers of each race employed in a particular occupation (e.g., 12 white carpenters at $2.00 per day, 3 black carpenters at $1.75 per day). The samples analyzed cover 290 firms making 490 contracts in 1900, and 636 firms making 1,595 contracts in 1909; they include 5,292 workers (2,247 white) in 1900 and 13,995 (6,937 white) in 1909. In view of the variety of occupations and the large number of firms, contracts, and workers represented, the sample provides a firm basis for generalizations.

Did a sample firm pay less to its black than to its white laborers? To answer this question, of course, one must examine only firms that actually hired both races in a given occupation. Table 4 shows the number of sample contracts covering integrated occupational workforces, distributed according to whether they paid whites more, both races the same, or blacks more. In 1900, 36 percent of the contracts paid whites more, 61 percent paid both races the same, and 3 percent paid blacks more; in 1909 the respective percentages were 38, 57, and 5. Clearly, from the standpoint of firm behavior, equal payment within a given occupation was the most common practice. In the absence of information on the skills, experience, and other productivity attributes of the workers within a given occupation, one cannot say whether the instances where a firm paid more to blacks or to whites indicate discriminatory behavior.

One can gain further information on this question, however, by distinguishing occupations according to their prevailing requirements of skills and experience. Under the maintained hypothesis that the observed racial wage differentials reflected differentials in worker productivity in a situation where the whites were better trained and more experienced on the average, one could predict that racial differentials would be more commonly observed in skilled occupations than in unskilled occupations. In the latter there is simply relatively little potential for productivity-associated heterogeneity in the workforce. When

TABLE 4 Distribution of Sample Contracts for Hire of Integrated Occupational Workforces, by Racial Difference in Wages Paid, Virginia, 1900 and 1909

| | Number of contracts paying: | | | |
| | Both same | Whites more | Blacks more | Total contacts |
Occupation				
1900				
Carpenters[a]	12	1	2	15
Lathers[a]	4	2	0	6
Brickmakers[a]	4	0	0	4
Tannery beamsmen[a]	0	7	1	8
Plumbing laborers	3	11	0	14
Sawmill teamsters	2	9	0	11
Loggers	2	4	0	6
Sawmill laborers	8	15	0	23
Bark grinders	1	6	0	7
Tannery yardmen	2	6	0	8
Tannery misc. help	2	6	0	8
Totals	40	67	3	110
1909				
Brickmakers[a]	8	5	0	13
Brickworks kilnmen[a]	4	2	0	6
Bricklayers[a]	6	2	0	8
Carpenters[a]	15	0	0	15
Sawmill engineers[a]	5	8	0	13
Sawyers[a]	3	4	1	8
Brickworks laborers	4	6	2	12
Bricklayer helpers	1	0	0	1
General contract laborers	14	19	7	40
Plumbing laborers	2	13	1	16
Sawmill laborers	14	44	1	59
Loggers	5	17	0	22
Sawmill misc. help	11	13	0	24
Sawmill teamsters	8	16	0	24
Totals	100	149	12	261

[a] Occupation classified as skilled or semiskilled.

Source: Robert Higgs, "Firm-Specific Evidence on Racial Wage Differentials and Workforce Segregation," *American Economic Review,* LXVII (March, 1977), 240.

the contracts are distributed according to the skill levels of the occupations, the results are as shown below.

	Occupations	
In 1900:	*skilled*	*unskilled*
Contracts paying blacks same or more	13	57
Contracts paying whites more	20	20
In 1909:		
Contracts paying blacks same or more	22	139
Contracts paying whites more	41	59

Obviously, the sample firms were much more likely to pay whites more than blacks in the skilled occupations. While this result does not justify rejection of the hypothesis that at least some firms paid purely discriminatory premiums to whites, the data are also consistent with the hypothesis that racial wage differentials reflected productivity differentials; and the latter hypothesis explains something that the former does not, namely, the much greater frequency of differentially higher wages paid to whites in the skilled occupations, where the whites ranked higher in terms of skills and experience on the average.

Even if white employers *paid* blacks and whites the same for the same work—which, of course, they did not always—black workers, on average, even within a given occupation, generally *received* lower wages than whites. There is no sleight of hand here; nor am I talking about the fraudulent withholding of wages. The discrepancy arose because black and white workers were distributed differently among firms paying different wage rates. A disproportionate number of blacks worked for firms that paid all workers, both black and white, relatively low wages. The Virginia study, for example, found that even though a large majority of contracts paid blacks as much as whites, the average wage received by blacks was significantly lower in a large majority of the sample occupations. The same conclusion was reached in (Paul Norgren's) Appendix 6 to Gunnar Myrdal's *American Dilemma,* with regard to the southern lumber industry in 1939–1940:

> The hourly earnings tended to be somewhat lower for Negro than for white lumber workers. Such a difference usually appears even when Negroes and whites in the same occupational sub-group are compared. . . . This does not prove, however, that Negroes are paid less on an hourly basis when performing the same duties as white workers in the same establishments. . . . [T]he main reason why Negroes, by and large, have lower pay than whites is that they are relatively more concentrated in low wage work.[13]

This distributional difference has always been apparent in comparisons across occupations. My point is that it also existed *across firms within occupations.*

I am emphasizing this point heavily because it has important implications for the economic analysis of racial inequalities, both historically and at present. Earlier I noted that the neoclassical model of discrimination rests on the assumption that whites dislike physical proximity to blacks and will pay a price to avoid it. This implies that, unless nondiscriminating employers effectively compete it away, racial discrimination in the labor market will result in racial income inequalities because white employers pay a premium to their white workers in integrated workforces; it will also result in integrated white workers' receiving higher wages than segregated white workers. Both of these predictions are generally refuted by the Virginia study of firm-specific evidence.[14] These findings suggest that many southern employers valued wealth more than discrimination and that competition did effectively transpire. Yet, after all this, blacks still collected lower average wages than whites in a given occupation and occupied themselves disproportionately in low-wage jobs. Why?

Part of the answer, obviously, is that the whites collectively denied blacks access to certain industries and occupations, using intimidation and threats of violence to enforce the exclusions. Clearly, employment discrimination was more significant than wage discrimination. The textile and furniture industries employed whites almost exclusively. Occupations such as electrician or plumber provided almost no openings for blacks. Municipal, county, and state governments seldom hired blacks except as unskilled laborers or as teachers in the segregated schools. We are all aware of how certain trade unions excluded blacks both from apprenticeships and from opportunities to learn from experience on the job. In the textile industry the extensive employment of white women heightened white sexual anxieties and led to exclusion of blacks from jobs as operatives for so-called "social" reasons. All of this was no doubt important, but it is too familiar to require restatement. Further, I believe its importance has probably been overstated at the expense of another, rather neglected consideration.

The neglected factor is that the black population occupied an initially disadvantaged position—geographically, educationally, and otherwise—and therefore bore a *disproportionate burden of adjustment* as the economic transformation of the South proceeded. To put it bluntly, if too simply, industrialization and urbanization did not occur in the Black Belt. Black people had to migrate farther than whites, on the average, to reach the growth centers of the South. Also, economic modernization continually increased the demand for literate and skilled workers; and again, the burden of adjustment weighed most heavily on the blacks, who suffered educationally from the legacy of enforced ignorance under slavery and from the continuing racial discrimination exercised by the segregated public school systems of the South. The whites of the Piedmont reaped a windfall gain, in a sense, when industrialization *came to them*. In Texas and Oklahoma, a similar windfall benefited a predominantly white subregional economy when the underground treasure of oil was discovered. For the blacks, to grasp the emerging opportunities seemed almost always to require relatively more investment: to migrate to the cities or to the North; to finance a decent education out of their own pockets; to establish a business for lack of a chance to participate in existing white enterprises. At the same time, the relatively high rates of natural increase prevailing in the rural Black Belt kept replacing the disadvantaged population even while many were migrating away from the area. Hence, the required adjustments became even greater. In view of the tremendous burdens of adjustment required and the persistent discriminatory obstacles placed in the path of these adjustments, I consider it quite remarkable that between 1900 and 1950 the blacks somehow managed almost to hold their own in the developing southern economy.

Racial discrimination assumed many guises in the South. But its main objective, to keep the blacks at large subordinate to the whites at large, was consistent with racial equality in some respects. In particular, white dominance in general did not preclude white employers from paying the same wages for the same work in the same establishment. Indeed, competition generally required that such equality prevail in integrated workforces. Collectively enforced exclusions, however, kept integrated workforces from appearing in many occupations. In addition, heavy burdens of adjustment hampered black economic progress and left blacks receiving lower wages *on average* even though *most* white employers probably did not practice racial wage discrimination.

The racial sensitivities of white employees could usually be placated by organizing segregated workforces, even if each gang performed the same task for the same pay. Workforce segregation was certainly common throughout the South: in the Virginia sample, for example, 71 percent of the whites and 50 percent of the blacks worked in segregated occupational workforces. But much of this segregation occurred because workforces were often small, hence easily segregated "by accident," especially in local labor markets with a preponderance of potential employees belonging to one race. Larger occupational workforces tended to be more frequently integrated, as employers sometimes found it intolerably costly to accommodate the hostilities of the white workers.[15] But any little racial distinction might be enough to satisfy the white workers, and it is virtually impossible to establish that such distinctions were not being made. Even if they were, however, their importance was more symbolic than substantial. The important thing was that an employer actually hired members of both races for the same occupation. That the whites might be given a highfalutin' job title did little harm to black workers so long as they received equal pay.

The existence of a segregated "Group Economy," as W. E. B. Du Bois called it, also provided a limited outlet for those blacks who would otherwise have found themselves in the unacceptable position of giving orders or advice to white people. In the Group Economy could be found virtually the entire entrepreneurial and professional class of the black labor force. Teachers, preachers, doctors, lawyers, storekeepers, building contractors, real estate brokers—all found the bulk, and often the entirety, of their clientele among the black population. Dewey's First Law apparently held with few exceptions in the South before 1950. Unfortunately, the Group Economy was doomed to fail from the start. It offered only pathetically constricted opportunities for the most part. Despite its natural appeal to racially oppressed people, the Group Economy served more to channel blacks into a dead end than as an avenue to opportunities in the larger economy.[16]

In summary, we have assessed two hypotheses and concluded

that each has general validity. The first is that pure wage discrimination was uncommon. The second is that blacks were concentrated, as a result of employment discrimination, either in jobs where they gave no orders nor advice to whites, or in segregated workforces, or in the segregated Group Economy. All of this added up to a heavy set of constraints, especially for people occupying an initially disadvantaged position and hence subject to disproportionately high costs of adjustment in seeking new economic opportunities. Not surprisingly, many students of black economic history have heavily stressed the notion of a vicious circle. Yet some opportunities were grasped; change did occur. We must still consider, then, our third hypothesis: that color lines and black earnings moved back and forth as population movements altered the racial composition of the labor market. In considering this hypothesis, we must confront the dynamics of change and adjustment that linked race and economy in the South during the first half of the twentieth century.

Dynamics of Disequilibrium and Adjustment
Economists have long found it useful to employ in their analysis the concept of equilibrium and to view economic changes as adjustments to disequilibrium. For example, if the wage rate prevailing in a labor market brings forth exactly the amount of labor services that employers wish to hire, then that wage rate is an equilibrium rate: every worker who wants to work at that wage rate can find employment, and every employer who wants to hire laborers at that wage rate can secure as many as he wants. No one has any incentive to change his behavior. Employers continue to offer and workers continue to accept the going wage rate, which, as the economists say, "clears the market."

Now suppose that something alters the situation, for example, that many workers migrate away from the area. In this case, the labor supply has shrunk; fewer workers now wish to work at the prevailing wage rate. But employers still wish to hire as many as before. This is a situation of disequilibrium, of so-called "excess demand for labor." Employers will discover that they can hire more workers, to replace the ones who moved away, only by offering a higher wage rate; at the same time, the remaining workers will discover that they can do better than before and will refuse to work at the old wage rate. The outcome of this adjustment process is that *eventually* a new equilibrium will be established: fewer workers will be employed than before, and the new prevailing wage rate will be higher than before. The labor market will accommodate itself, so to speak, to the new reality of a smaller labor force.

Economic theory has little to say about how long it takes to move from one equilibrium to another or about exactly what happens during the transition period. The adjustment to dis-equilibrium, however, comprises much of the behavior of prime concern to historians, sociologists, politicians, and ordinary people. The adjustment may include social protests, political struggles, personal and group conflicts, violence, suffering, hero-ism, cruelty, and all sorts of human difficulties, triumphs, and tragedies. The economist contents himself in the knowledge that the outcome of all this kicking and squealing is foreordained. But the actors in the human drama often learn slowly and struggle vigorously against the inevitable.

It is often useful to view the adjustment to economic disequilibrium as occurring in two stages, even though the two normally overlap. In Stage I, those placed at a disadvantage by the disequilibrium refuse to adjust in the economic sense and resort instead to coercive devices in an attempt to preserve the *status quo ante*. To continue with the labor market example, employers initially refuse to raise the wage rate; instead, they attempt to stem the tide of out-migration and to force resident laborers to continue working at the long-established wage rate. They are likely to view that wage rate as endowed with moral sanction; it is, they may say, "all the labor is worth." Laborers, of course, resent attempts at coercion and resist them. If their resistance is effective, then at least some employers will necessarily have to choose between raising the wage rate and doing without labor altogether. Under these circumstances, the wage rate will be bid up. This is Stage II, which terminates when the wage rate has been raised to the point where it again clears the market. To the extent that coercion is relatively effective, Stage I will last a long time. Once it has passed, Stage II may run its course rather quickly.

This general approach to the analysis of adjustment to disequilibrium applies especially well to historical events involving white employers and black employees in the South. Coercion, after all, was always an option when the whites dealt with the blacks. But careful analysts have recognized that competitive pressures also played a significant role. Since emancipation, it has been impossible for the whites to rely *exclusively* on force and violence. (Some scholars contend that it was impossible even under slavery.) The more immobile, ignorant, and isolated the blacks, the more could the whites rely on coercion. Between 1890 and 1950, however, these characteristics evolved considerably in favor of the blacks. Increased literacy, greater mobility, and urbanization all contributed toward shortening or eliminating altogether the adjustments of Stage I type. Increased interregional flows of communication and publicity, and political and legal conditions imposed on the South by the rest of the country had the same effect.

One can find much evidence of the trend. The decline of lynchings is indicative. I am not suggesting that many lynchings necessarily had any connection with economic disequilibrium, but I do suspect that the frequency of lynchings is an index of the extent to which white southerners resorted to violence on other occasions in their dealings with blacks. During the 1890s, the number of blacks lynched per year averaged 116, or about one every third day! From its peak in the early 1890s, the trend of lynchings was unmistakably downward. By the late 1930s, lynchings had become almost rare, with fewer than 10 blacks per year dying at the hands of mobs.[17] No doubt many influences contributed to the decline of this savage conduct, and I am not qualified to say what all of them were. My hunch, however, is that the dramatic decline of lynchings paralleled a similar decline in the frequency with which whites resorted to force and violence in dealing with blacks in situations of economic disequilibrium.

The example of labor market disequilibrium earlier discussed is illustrative of a situation that became chronic in the South between 1915 and 1930 and again during the 1940s. Blacks were migrating out of the region in large numbers. When the Great Migration first got under way, the response of the whites was indeed to resort to coercion rather than to economic adjustments. As Emmett Scott described it, "[D]rastic legislation and force were employed. In Alabama, Arkansas, Mississippi and Georgia laws were passed in an effort to suppress the activities of labor agents. Licenses were made prohibitively high; labor agents were arrested and heavily fined. In some cases their coming was penalized to prohibit their operations entirely and they frequently suffered physical injury."[18]

In many places police made mass arrests of migrants congregating at southern railway stations, holding them on various trumped-up charges in an attempt at intimidation. All such efforts failed to deter the migrants; in fact, such coercion only hardened their resolve. The whites then tried reconciliation and persuasion, which were cheap but ineffective means of slowing the exodus. Stage II was about to begin. Wages started to climb throughout the South, quickly doubling and even

trebling in some places. Scott insightfully described the adjustment process and its spill-over effects on racial relations.

Throughout the South there was not only a change in policy as
to the method of stopping the migration of the blacks to the
North, but a change in the economic policy of the South. Southern business men and planters soon found out that it was impossible to treat the negro as a serf and began to deal with him as
an actual employe entitled to his share of the returns from his
labor. . . . There was, too, a decided change in the attitude
of the whole race toward the blacks. . . . Instead of expressing
their indignation at such efforts on the part of the negroes, the
whites listened to them attentively. . . . White men, for the
first time, were talking on the streets with negroes just as white
men talk with each other. The merchants gave their negro
patrons more attention and consideration. . . . The suspension
of harsh treatment was so marked in some places that few
negroes neglected to mention it. . . . The tendency to maltreat
the negroes without cause, the custom of arresting them for petty
offenses and the institution of lynching have all been somewhat
checked by this change in the attitude of the southern white man
towards the negro.[19]

Scott may have painted this portrait in excessively rosy hues,
but its general features were true to life. It would be difficult
to find a better illustration of the two-stage adjustment to economic disequilibrium or of the close interrelation of race and
economy in the South.

When another great migration began during the 1940s, the
Stage 1 adjustments were much briefer and less painful. The
South had become a more economic, which is to say a less
savage, society. And it is clear that the increased literacy,
knowledge, mobility, wealth, and urbanization of the black
population contributed heavily toward this result. Ultimately, the
transformation of the southern economy from a relatively static,
rural, and agricultural organization to a dynamic urban-industrial
form had provided the main precondition for a more civilized

system of racial relations. The battle was by no means won in 1950. Indeed, many at that time could perceive little change in the South's traditional system of racial relations. But the foundations of that system had been irreparably undermined, and it was at last possible to envision its eventual destruction.

The Cost of Segregation

GEORGE B. TINDALL

A symposium on the Age of Segregation is itself an extended statement on the cost of segregation. Any further effort to tabulate the costs, therefore, is apt to turn into a dreary audit of accounts long since rendered, if still unsettled. Almost ninety years ago, in fact, a Virginian named Lewis Harvie Blair, a Richmond businessman, submitted a cost-estimate that anticipated most of the major items since entered on the books. He did it even before the system of segregation with its attendant burdens of disfranchisement, repression, and dependence had yet fully congealed into the new peculiar institution of the twentieth century.

Blair's book bore an unwieldy title, *The Prosperity of the South Dependent Upon the Elevation of the Negro* (1889), but the title nonetheless summarized his argument aptly.[1] Among "many causes conspiring to the poverty or lack of prosperity of the South . . . ," he wrote, "a greater and more far-reaching cause of all is the degradation of the Negro. . . . Like a malignant cancer which poisons the whole system, this degradation seems to intensify all the other drawbacks under which we labor."

Like the novelist George Washington Cable, the most prominent among his few counterparts of that day, Blair sought to animate the white man's sense of justice, but unlike Cable, he rested his case mainly on an appeal to self-interest. In effect Blair expanded on Booker T. Washington's point that you cannot keep a man down in a ditch without staying down there with him.

Blair's iconoclasm spared few of the racial shibboleths of the times. As to segregation, he wrote: "The Negro must be allowed free access to all hotels and other places of public entertainment." As to voting, he said: "this is the right preservative of all rights." As to education: "Separate schools poison at its very source the stream whence spring the best and noblest fruits of education." Blair remained, of course, a prophet without honor in his own day, and in fact himself succumbed to the fashion of racism before he died, but on many pages his words still speak to the concerns of another day. "The whites," he wrote, "are dominated by a great apprehension—namely, that the elevation of the Negro means the degradation of the whites —and until this fear is allayed . . . , it will be like appealing to the winds to urge them to steps leading to the complete elevation . . . of the Negro."

Other writers over the years extended the ledger of shame and deprivation which Lewis Blair drew up. Relatively few of them, however, were historians. In 1954, when the time came for the Supreme Court to decide the school segregation cases, the justices leaned heavily on the findings of the sociologists and psychologists for their decision. Historical findings were conspicuous by their absence from the citations in the famous footnote eleven of the opinion. "Perhaps that was just as well," Philip D. Swenson wrote in a recent interview. "Had the Warren Court turned to Clio, it would have been profoundly disappointed."[2]

The lawyers for the NAACP, in fact, *had* turned to Clio and *had* been profoundly disappointed. A team of historians enlisted to examine the origins of the Fourteenth Amendment turned up little that was germane one way or the other. Such a focus perhaps was beside the point, since it would have required no miraculous revelation from the muse to disclose that, whatever the framers of the amendment had intended, "separate but equal" had seldom if ever been more than a legal fiction to gloss over the shabbiness of Jim Crow facilities—and often their absence. In the light of experience, a belief that separate could be equal required a leap of faith as great as a belief that literacy tests for voting had something to do with literacy.

It would be all too easy to recite the dreary ledger of shame and hardship which Blair began and scholars are still extending, but there may be some question whether anything is to be gained from dancing on the grave of Jim Crow any longer. If, indeed, the celebration is not still premature.

Other times bring other needs, and perspectives have a way of shifting. In the thirty years since Vernon Wharton published *The Negro in Mississippi, 1865–1890* (1947), one measure of the distance we have come is the difficulty one would have in recapturing the sense of discovery that came to a generation of historians who learned that the Age of Segregation in which they grew up dated from somewhat later than remote antiquity.[3] The discovery had an obvious relevance to the challenges then being mounted against the *Plessy* doctrine. If segregation was an institution of comparatively recent origin, and if laws and stateways had played a significant part in creating it, then laws and stateways might be used to change or destroy it. Whatever effect they might have on hearts and minds, if laws and stateways could alter human behavior in one direction, they could alter it in another.

Such connections, of course, might skew historical judgments, for they held out a temptation to exaggerate the extent or warmth of interracial contacts that had preceded the "deep freeze" of the early twentieth century. David Potter once observed in this very connection that a historian may experience "an inner struggle in which his historical realism [is] pitted against his liberal urge to find constructive meanings in the past for the affairs of the present."[4] And however well the historian might resolve such a struggle, readers subject to wishful thinking could find themselves drawn to the illusion of a romantic golden age that had never existed.

And the challenge to segregation had a deceptive clarity of focus. To quote the title of Richard Kluger's recent narrative of events leading to the *Brown* decision, it was a question of *Simple Justice*.[5] We now know, however, that the road to simple justice led on into a tangled thicket of complexity: pupil placement, freedom of choice, interposition, massive resistance, segregated academies, affirmative action, guidelines, quotas and goals, reverse discrimination, black separatism, white flight— until one becomes entangled in a dense undergrowth of mutual suspicion, the heritage of a past that would not die easily.

Not least among the costs of segregation, perhaps, was the way in which it functioned as the most visible symbol of a far broader culture complex of prejudice and discrimination. As such it became the prime target of attack, and thus narrowed the focus of historical investigation and controversy. The attention of historians fixed on the origins of segregation, and more specifically on dating the origins. At first new findings more often than not confirmed the interpretation that placed the onset of the "deep freeze" at the turn of the century, an idea most cogently expressed in C. Vann Woodward's *The Strange Career of Jim Crow*.[6] But later students of race relations in the northern states discovered examples of segregation there before the Civil War. Others found examples in the antebellum South.

Then, in a study of postbellum South Carolina, Joel Williamson asserted: "Well before the end of Reconstruction, segregation had crystallized into a comprehensive pattern which, in its essence, remained unaltered until the middle of the twentieth century." There may have been exceptions in practice, but "the pattern of separation was fixed in the minds of the whites almost simultaneously with the emancipation of the Negro."[7] Such an interpretation, however, seems not entirely incompatible with the earlier findings. Whatever existed inside the heads of South Carolinians, their practices underwent a significant change at the turn of the century.

We can now safely say, however, that the strange career of the historical controversy over the origins of segregation has just about run its course and exhausted its potential for further enlightenment. What is needed, Vann Woodward suggested in *American Counterpoint,* is "a theory, a model, perhaps a typology of race relations that would conceive of the historical problem of segregation not as one of dating origins at a point in linear time but of accounting for the phenomenon in whatever degree it appears."[8] Woodward called attention especially to theories derived from comparative history and sociology by Pierre L. van den Berghe and Philip Mason, who between them draw upon observation and study in the strange ethnic borderlands of five continents.[9]

One constant in race relations has been conceptions of dominance and subordination, but these authors have noted successive stages of development which parallel the evolution from what classic sociology called *Gemeinschaft* to *Gesellschaft,* that is, from a traditional society of personal relations to a society in which human relations are more complex and impersonal. Both authors see a movement from social distance to physical distance in the definition of racial status and roles: in van den Berghe's terms, from paternalism to competition; in Mason's, from certainty to challenge and rivalry. Mason, moreover, goes on to a third stage: concessions by the dominant group which may be met by "a profound refusal to accept what has long been withheld."[10]

The quest for universal laws of history, however, like the

quest for central themes, tends to be confounded by the innate perversity of human nature. One of the longest established games in comparative history has been the exploration of the two largest slave societies in the New World: the American South and the Brazilian North. The exercise, however, has fairly consistently suggested at least as much contrast as comparison—more often than not to the advantage of Brazil. The aforementioned Lewis Blair, for example, quoted a Virginian who in the 1850s had served as consul at Rio, where he found one of the emperor's ministers and one of the court physicians to be "black Negroes." Many of the blacks he had met at parties and receptions, the former consul said, "educated in Europe and favored with wealth, were much more elegantly cultured than he was himself."[11] Other travelers to Brazil had reported similar observations even earlier, and scholars in both countries have explored them in the twentieth century.

It is often noted that one key difference in Brazilian race relations has been the recognition of gradations in pigmentation and other physical characteristics. The United States has what Joel Williamson called in South Carolina a "duo-chromatic order"—one is either black or white. As a character in one of Langston Hughes's novels put it, black blood is powerful: "One drop—you are a Negro! Now, why is that? Why is Negro blood so much more powerful than any other kind of blood in the world?"[12]

Brazil, on the other hand, has had what might be called a "multichromatic order"—one may be black, white, or any of several shades between. Carl Degler alludes to this in the title of his book *Neither Black nor White*, in which he notes what has often been noted before but with a new emphasis and a different twist.[13] Brazilians, he acknowledges, have not strongly opposed racial mixing and have indeed taken pride in their multichromatic order. But what has less often been emphasized, Degler notes, is a subtle gradation of prejudice and discrimination more or less corresponding to the scale of color. Despite public disavowals and standards flexible enough to accommodate exceptions, the existence of such a scale makes a difference in the individual's standing and self-esteem.

And it yields a fine irony. Brazilian attitudes made emancipation a less traumatic if more prolonged experience there than in the United States, but then served to mask subtle discrimination behind claims of racial democracy. The presence of what Degler calls "the mulatto escape hatch" lent credibility to the claims of racial democracy, but at the expense of unity in resisting discriminations. Sharp distinctions of color in the United States, on the other hand, served both to make discrimination more visible and to unite all people of black ancestry with a sense of common identity. Brazil, therefore, has had no civil rights movement comparable to that in the United States.

Work in comparative history has broadened perspectives of time as well as geography. In one of the new contributions to the history of the period, for instance, in a book on *Race Relations in the Urban South, 1865–1890*, Howard Rabinowitz explores the transition from the Age of Slavery to the Age of Segregation and suggests that racial segregation itself was a kind of evolutionary advancement after all.[14] At first that may sound just too outrageous to credit. But the first impression may come from a natural tendency to read history backward instead of forward. Today we tend to think of the alternatives as segregation versus integration. And the onset of segregation shattered the hopes of integration that had been raised during Reconstruction. But the fact was that the hopes seldom approached reality even during Reconstruction. New Orleans, for instance, was the only community in the South that made any serious attempt at integrated schools, and that experiment was soon brought to a screeching halt.

If we take the trouble to go back with Howard Rabinowitz and read history forward, we find that (in his words) "the emphasis on the alternatives of segregation or integration has obscured the obvious 'forgotten alternative' which was not integration, but exclusion. The issue, therefore, should not be merely when segregation first appeared, but what it replaced. For in the beginning—which is to say before the Civil War— blacks were excluded from the franchise, militia companies, schools, and most hospitals, asylums, and places of public accommodation. . . . Nevertheless, by 1890 . . . *de facto* segregation had replaced exclusion as the norm in southern race relations. In the process the stage of integration had been largely skipped."[15] Still, however paradoxical it seems today, even segregation opened doors that had once been closed entirely. Segregated schools, however poorly supported, were something other than no schools at all. But segregation of course failed to open all the doors, and failed to open any of them all the way.

There are still other entries to be made on the credit side of our historical ledger—and some that will be more readily apparent than that one. We know, of course, that behind what W. E. B. Du Bois called the veil of segregation there grew up a group economy of black businessmen, publishers, editors, merchants, entertainers, teachers, ministers, doctors, and other professionals who served a kind of protected market in the black community. A growing response to segregation and disfranchisement was to make a virtue of necessity. It was a matter of "taking advantage of our disadvantages," as Booker T. Washington once put it. Separate enterprises, separate churches, separate colleges afforded a training ground for leadership largely insulated from white control, and thus afforded also chances to organize against the barriers of segregation. The great historical irony was that the institution of segregation nurtured the seeds of its own destruction.

In the separate world of black America there grew up also an ethnic folk culture as rich as any in human experience.[16]

Black humor and music and folklore served black people as a psychological instrument of survival and eventually made important contributions to the high arts. Out of a rich and diverse heritage the black community generated a new musical idiom, jazz, which can make claim to being the most original and perhaps the only truly original American contribution to the arts.

On the other side of the color line were a white elite who thrived in a world of deference and low wages and whose interests benefited from domination and even from a certain level of racial tension. "Sustained racial passions," George Mowry has written, "meant one-party government, one-party government meant upper-class control, and hence antiunion government, Q. E. D.: a certain level of racial animosity worked to the benefit of the owning classes."[17] One need not embrace a conspiracy theory of deliberate agitation to acknowledge the validity of Mowry's point, although examples of such can be adduced. The gains that might be derived by a few from the maintenance of a colonial economy, however, would have to be balanced against the impediments to innovation and economic development which still persist. Evidence from the recent Age of Black Revolt, nevertheless, suggests that political ambition could tolerate a higher level of racial animosity than the profit motive. When push came to shove, the chambers of commerce, by and large, preferred to make concessions.

If there are some tentative points to be made on the credit side, some dubious returns from segregation, perhaps we should just admit an instinctive hankering to find a little bit of good in every bit of bad, and let it go at that. Surely, after two decades of debate on the profitability of slavery and three years of *Time on the Cross*, we might hope to be spared yet another great debate on the profitability of segregation. But one is already well on the way. Until recently it has been just a cloud on the horizon, one that has precipitated a few articles here and there, mainly in the *Journal of Economic History,* a book by Stephen De Canio, another by Professor Robert Higgs, yet another by Roger Ransom and Richard Sutch.[18]

Faced with this impending flood, some of you may feel impelled to head for high ground. For those who are willing to ride it out, I would suggest as a lifeline an article by Harold D. Woodman, "Sequel to Slavery: The New History Views the Postbellum South," in the *Journal of Southern History.*[19] So far much of the controversy I fear, may be headed toward another confirmation of George Bernard Shaw's observation that, if all the economists in the world were laid end to end, they would not reach a conclusion.

The wellspring of this flood seems to have been a University of Chicago dissertation by Gary Becker, first published in 1957 as *The Economics of Discrimination.*[20] The argument, if an unreconstructed humanist can judge aright, depends first upon the classical model of a free market within which the actors are motivated by self-interest. Prejudice, however, may give the participants a "taste for discrimination," a luxury for which they may be prepared to pay, like other luxuries. Others, however, may have a less developed taste for discrimination and will bid up the price of black labor. The effect of their actions (and theoretically one is enough) is to force the hand of the others. Thus, all things work to good for them that trust *The Wealth of Nations.*

When one is first confronted with the proposition that discrimination is quantifiable, one may be forgiven for feeling that, like a stage play, the proposition requires a certain willing suspension of disbelief. Some of the new findings verge on the principle—or so it seems to a mind untutored in mathematics— that if you can develop an equation which excludes most of the impact of racial discrimination, then you have an equation which minimizes discrimination. Of course, in all fields one must isolate certain things for purposes of analysis, but in this

particular thicket of economic history one begins to suspect that
not all economists have a good sense of algorithm. Or rather
that they sometimes ignore most of the forest and take to bark-
ing up the wrong binary tree. In any case, the unreconstructed
humanist who cannot cope with coefficients will stand indebted
to cliometricians like Robert Higgs who affirm that English is
a language too and who, while they focus on one part of the
forest, do acknowledge the existence of another part of the
forest.

For a time the thesis of Gary Becker got only passing notice,
and acquired disciples only with the most deliberate speed.
For the most part the historical quantifiers were obsessed with
the profitability of slavery, but some began to venture into the
reconstructed world of sharecropping and the lien system. The
first book-length contribution, Stephen De Canio's *Agriculture
in the Postbellum South*, strongly challenged the conventional
wisdom on several major points. The farmers' persistence in
growing cotton struck De Canio as an optimum use of resources,
given the available alternative, corn. He seemed unwilling to
consider other alternatives, but given the way tenancy, credit,
and habit conspired to force the shotgun marriage of cotton
and corn, perhaps there was no other alternative. Second, De
Canio argued that farm labor was not exploited but received
income somewhat above its marginal product. Finally, although
white cotton farmers fared best of all in the postbellum South,
black farmers as a whole fared better than white noncotton
farmers, differences explained mainly by the quality of the soil
on which they were located.

De Canio's results, he argues, "conclusively eliminate the
naive 'legacy of slavery' notion that blacks as a whole were less
productive than whites as a whole because they were deprived
of human capital." They were, however, deprived of other
forms of capital. "A major source of economic equality and
relative poverty was the same as in any normally functioning

private enterprise market economy—incomes were unequal largely because of unequal ownership of the nonhuman factors of production."[21] That point remains unexplored largely because it is beyond the reach of econometrics. But is that not perhaps the crucial point?

Robert Higgs, in his recent book *Competition and Coercion: Blacks in the American Economy, 1865–1914*, assumes a broader perspective. He emphasizes again the relative absence of wage discrimination in the marketplace. On the other hand, he never loses sight of the debit side of the ledger (the *Coercion* of his title), but calls attention once again to some of the credits— and thereby reinforces the Rabinowitz point that, whatever legacy of slavery remained, certain gains were achieved and certain doors were opened, most significantly the doors to literacy and migration, the latter a force of massive consequence in the twentieth century, politically as well as economically. What is more, growing skills and experience in farm management, the trades (Higgs to some extent discounts the old story of the displacement of black artisans), and entry into business and the professions all led to better paying jobs, in some cases to self-employment, and by 1900 to a per capita income about double that of the late 1860s.

Another recent contribution to the growing flood of literature on the subject is a book by Roger Ransom and Richard Sutch, *One Kind of Freedom: The Economic Consequences of Emancipation*, which has been foretokened in several articles. The authors' argument might be summarized, if somewhat inadequately, as updating and rounding out Lewis H. Blair's southern prophecy of some ninety years ago. The flawed economy of the post–Civil War South, they argue, was a direct heritage of slavery and racial discrimination, a system in which the merchants' monopoly of credit stymied innovation and development. At first the freedmen were subjected to the new bondage of sharecropping, but as time went by the marginal white farmers were drawn into the vortex as well. In a sense it may have been the best of all possible worlds, given the tragic legacy of the past, but in the long run it was a stagnant world in which the routines of sharecropping and tenancy, the crop lien, and the commodity markets yielded only with difficulty to other possibilities—ultimately only to the shock of outside forces: the massive invasion of the boll weevil and the massive exodus of the blacks in the Great Migration. For a long time the one-crop system, the impediments to capital formation, and the barriers to migration were severe encumbrances, but in the words of Ransom and Sutch: "As a cause of southern poverty, racism may well have been preeminent," a force which permeated society, distorted economic institutions, blighted hopes, and pursued blacks on into the marketplace for urban labor.[22]

The econometric debate, to adopt a somewhat occult metaphor, seems to have conjured up a kind of spooky test of strength between the dead hand of tradition and the invisible hand of Adam Smith. It is reassuring to be told that forces in the marketplace worked against discrimination and at least afforded some chance for a rough equality of rewards to those able to make roughly equal contributions of labor. But, granting this much for the sake of argument, it would be another thing to be told that the invisible hand of competition could exorcise the dead hand of racism which haunted an entire culture. Professor Higgs and others do grant the drastic obstacles that confronted blacks before they reached the marketplace, obstacles so great as to exclude them from some parts of the market. "The fountainhead of effective discrimination," Professor Higgs has written, ". . . lay in the governments of the Southern states, counties, and cities, where the racial monopoly of politics allowed the hostile whites to treat the blacks as they pleased."[23]

But there were other fountainheads of such power: economic, social, and cultural. In some of the other new studies which

Harold Woodman has spied out on the horizon, perspectives seem to be broadening into a grand reassessment of their force. If Ransom and Sutch have come full circle back to Blair's southern prophecy, other studies seem to be coming full circle back to the perspective of Rupert Vance, who in 1929 launched his scholarly career with *Human Factors in Cotton Culture,* an extensive description and analysis of a one-crop culture complex which held millions in bondage to poverty and ignorance.[24] Vance brought to bear on the subject a broad erudition not only in his own field of sociology but also geography, economics, literature, and other disciplines. It is worth noting parenthetically, perhaps, that in 1965, on the eve of his retirement, Vance produced an article, "Beyond the Fleshpots," in which he pronounced the Mason-Dixon line "no longer . . . an iron curtain against the Affluent Society."[25] The linkage of cause and effect between the South's emergence from poverty (if not yet to economic parity with the nation) and the emergence from segregation may offer a further chance in the future to test the interpretations with which we are now being swamped. The emergence from political isolation will need to be factored in as well.

But for the moment it will be more than enough to cope with the social histories which are coming onstream. Woodman tells us that Jonathan M. Wiener and Jay R. Mandle now have on the way studies which will explore much the same ground as the cliometricians but from the perspective of social history and particularly the effort of a planter class to preserve its hegemony and its control over land and labor, an effort which they see as generally successful, and finally evolving into an alliance with a new capitalist elite of merchants, bankers, and factory masters.[26] Both V. O. Key and George Mowry—as well as many others—have suggested that there has existed in southern society a power elite which has remained little studied and little understood. This is one of the next tasks in southern history—

the study of race, class, and power. Who exercised power over whom, to what ends, and how?

In the study and writing of history, despite the broadening and deepening that has occurred in recent years, one cost of segregation still being paid is the focus on what white people did to black people at the expense of attention to the lives and achievements of black people themselves, the focus on blacks as victims at the expense of attention to blacks as builders and doers. In an essay contributed to the *Festschrift* for Fletcher Green twelve years ago, I suggested that the Age of Segregation had given rise to a peculiarly static image of Negro life. Black people seldom appeared in historical writing "as actors with vital roles or collectively as a positive social force." They appeared as "an undifferentiated background, as subjects to be acted upon, but not as people whose affairs have innate significance."[27]

At the end of that essay I cited Gunnar Myrdal's prognosis twenty years earlier that the long "period of stagnation was only a temporary balancing of forces which was just on the verge of being broken." I added that: "It does not require so bold a foresight to suggest that Negro historiography is only at the beginning of a similar release of forces. The next two decades will probably see an extensive historical invasion of areas that have long been forfeited to sociologists."[28] The events of subsequent years have borne out Myrdal's prophecy. One consequence of those events was that they brought the study of black history to the verge of a similar release of forces. With the end of that period of stagnation, it became far easier to see in perspective that beneath the apparently static surface of black life, something had been happening all along. New forces were gathering that would have a profound impact on the future.

To attempt at this point a survey of the new literature on black life—social, political, economic, educational, and religious —the state studies, the studies of intellectual history, the ethnic folk culture, and a host of other topics, to deal with all these here would extend these remarks beyond the limits of endurance. The publications are coming on so fast, in fact, that one can hardly keep up with the titles, much less digest the contents.

Besides, the coming two decades of which I wrote twelve years ago still have eight more years to run. By then, we shall have laid a good many historians as well as economists end to end. Perhaps by then the new findings with which we are now being swamped will have merged downstream into some grand new synthesis. But what it might be, to use the words of Alan Paton, why, that is a secret.

Notes

Notes to THE RACIAL IMPERATIVE IN AMERICAN LAW
by Derrick A. Bell, Jr.*

* Professor of Law, Harvard University. Ms. Susan Mentser, B.A. Swarth-
more, 1975, provided valuable research assistance for this lecture.
    1. Rayford Logan, The Betrayal of the Negro, from Rutherford B.
Hayes to Woodrow Wilson (1965), originally published as The Negro in
American Life and Thought: The Nadir, 1877–1901.
    2. Mary F. Berry suggests in Military Necessity and Civil Rights Policy
(1977) 104–106, that the Civil Rights Act of 1866 was the result of a search
for some legal way to settle the peacetime status of blacks, and put at ease
the still-armed black Union soldiers, most of whom were subsequently
transferred to the frontier or demobilized and largely disarmed. One wonders what the North's response would have been when the southern campaign of Redemption began, had black war veterans been able to resist the
Redeemer's attacks with weapons more effective than the generally un-
answered petitions for aid to the federal government.
    3. The courts generally refuse to hear such issues, claiming they are
"political questions" and not justiceable. See, e.g., Mora v. McNamara,
387 F.2d 862 (D.C. Cir. 1967), cert. denied, 389 U.S. 934 (1967),
(Douglas, J., dissenting from denial of certiorari); Atlee v. Laird, 347
F.Supp. 689 (E.D. Pa. 1972) (dismissal of suit to test constitutionality of
war in Southeast Asia), aff'd., 411 U.S. 911 (1973) (over the dissents of
Justices Douglas, Brennan, and Stewart). See generally, Anthony A.
D'Amato and Robert M. O'Neil, The Judiciary and Vietnam (1972), 51–59.
    4. Edmund Morgan, American Slavery, American Freedom (1975), joins
the growing group of his peers who find elements of both prejudice and
profit motivated the acceptance of slavery, with emphasis on the latter.
    5. John Hope Franklin, From Slavery to Freedom (4th ed.; 1974), 105;
Eugene Genovese, The Political Economy of Slavery (1961), 43–69.
    6. See Arthur Zilversmit, The First Emancipation, The Abolition of
Slavery in the North (1967); Winthrop Jordan, White over Black: American Attitudes Toward the Negro, 1550–1812 (1968), 345; Leon Litwack,
North of Slavery (1961), 3–29.

7. Amendment XIII, proposed January 31, 1865, declared ratified December 18, 1865; Amendment XIV, proposed June 13, 1866, declared ratified July 28, 1868; Article XV, proposed February 26, 1869 declared ratified March 30, 1870.

8. See Louis Filler, *The Crusade Against Slavery, 1830–1860* (1960), 82–96; Litwack, *North of Slavery*, 162–66.

9. For a discussion of the Compromise of 1877 and the Hayes-Tilden controversy, see C. Vann Woodward, *Reunion and Reaction* (1951); Paul Haworth, *The Hayes-Tilden Disputed Presidential Election of 1876* (1906), and Paul Buck, *The Road to Reunion, 1865–1900* (1938).

10. W. E. B. Du Bois pointed out in 1902 that the black artisan had fared better under slavery when white masters had managed their hiring arrangements, wage bargaining, and suing of creditors. Minus white protection after the Civil War, black artisans found it difficult to succeed in obtaining fair wages or even work. Poignantly, Du Bois saw the black mechanic's remedy in social protection "the protection of law and order, perfectly fair judicial processes and that personal power which is in the hands of all modern laboring classes in civilized lands, viz., the right of suffrage," all of which, of course, blacks failed to receive for the next fifty years. W. E. B. Du Bois (ed.), *The Negro Artisan, Report of a Social Study Made under the Direction of Atlanta University; Together with the Proceedings of the Seventh Conference for the Study of the Negro Problems* (1902) in *The Atlanta University Publications* (1969).

11. See Arnold Paul, *Conservative Crisis and the Rule of Law: Attitudes of Bar and Bench, 1887–1895* (1969), 19–81; Robert McCloskey, *American Conservatism in the Age of Enterprise* (1951), 72–126; Robert Harris, *The Quest for Equality* (1960), 57–108; and Charles Warren, *The Supreme Court in United States History* (1922), III, 255–343.

12. For a discussion of the major issues of the day, see C. Vann Woodward, *Origins of the New South* (1951), 369–95; Harold Faulkner, *The Quest for Social Justice, 1898–1914* (1931); Robert Wiebe, *The Search for Order 1877–1920* (1967).

13. See C. Vann Woodward, *The Strange Career of Jim Crow* 103 (3rd rev. ed.; 1974), 103; Logan, *Betrayal of the Negro*, 165–174; Thomas Gosset, *Race: The History of an Idea in America* (1963), 144–75, 253–309.

14. See discussion of northern newspapers' positions on suffrage issue, 1890–1901, in Logan, *Betrayal of the Negro*, 195–217. For other discussions of the suffrage issue in the North and West, see Forrest Wood, *Black Scare, The Racist Response to Emancipation and Reconstruction* (1968), 80–102; David Southern, *The Malignant Heritage: Yankee Progressives and the Negro Question 1901–1914* (1968), and Barbara Solomon, *Ancestors and Immigrants: A Changing New England Tradition* (1956).

15. The judges, as members of the legal profession, had had a legal education conservative in nature and had generally gone on to practice law for corporate powers. Thus their professional development took a conservative bent. Moreover, in its decisions, the Court had been generally called upon to preserve the status quo, to prevent either state or federal government from taking action. It had generally tended toward the

exercise of "negative power." See McCloskey, *American Conservatism in the Age of Enterprise*, 75–77.

16. E.g., Lochner v. New York, 198 U.S. 45 (1905) (business protected from state regulation); *In re* Debs, 158 U.S. 564 (1895) (denied rights to labor); Pollock v. Farmers Loan and Trust Co., 157 U.S. 429 (1895) (prohibition of federal income tax); and United States v. E. C. Knight Co., 156 U.S. (1895) (weakened Sherman Anti-Trust Act).

17. Reduction of privileges and immunities under federal protection: Slaughterhouse Cases, 83 U.S. (16 Wall.) 36 (1873); United States v. Reese, 92 U.S. 214 (1876); United States v. Cruikshank, 92 U.S. 542 (1876). Invalidation of public accommodation provisions: Civil Rights Cases, 109 U.S. 3 (1883). Formulation of separate but equal doctrine: Plessy v. Ferguson, 163 U.S. 537 (1896).

18. Failure to obtain such reassurance was a factor in the exodus of blacks from the South. For a remarkable account of southern violence and the subsequent migration of blacks to Kansas, see Nell Painter, *Exodusters: Black Migration to Kansas after Reconstruction* (1977). See also Robert Carr, *Federal Enforcement of Civil Rights: Quest for a Sword* (1947), 40–55.

19. See cases cited, notes 23 and 24, herein.

20. See Homer Cummings and Carl McFarland, *Federal Justice* (1937), 241–46. For an account of the extended period of violence in Louisiana, beginning in 1868, see Lerone Bennett, Jr., *Black Power U.S.A.: The Human Side of Reconstruction, 1867–1877* (1967), 251–57.

21. 92 U.S. 542 (1876). See Cummings and McFarland, *Federal Justice*, 241–46.

22. In United States v. Harris, 106 U.S. 629 (1882), the Ku Klux Act, which prohibited traveling the highways in disguise with the intent of denying certain citizens equal protection of the laws, was declared unconstitutional. United States v. Powell, 112 U.S. 564 (1908) affg. 151 Fed. 648 (C.C.N.D. Ala. 1907) concerned a mob who had taken a black accused of murder from a sheriff and a company of Alabama national guardsmen and had lynched him. Again the Supreme Court declared that since the act had been committed by individuals rather than the state or its officers, it could not intercede or punish the mob. Charles Mangum, Jr., *The Legal Status of the Negro* (1940), 288–89.

23. Woodward, *Origins*, 351.

24. Woodward, *Strange Career*, 114–15. Violence occurred despite the fact that 360,000 blacks were in the military during World War I. In the first year after the war, 70 blacks were lynched.

25. Pauli Murray, *States' Laws on Race and Color* (1950), 13; Franklin, *From Slavery to Freedom*, 362. The NAACP took up an asserted campaign against racial violence. In 1919, it held a national conference on lynching. By 1924, the organization had raised $45,000 to publicize its antilynching campaign and to defend blacks.

26. Woodward, *Origins*, 350.

27. During the campaign in 1890 for the election of delegates to Mississippi's constitutional convention, a black convention was held in order

to encourage the election of black delegates. Warnings to blacks to desist, at first issued through the newspapers, were later buttressed by the murder of a Republican candidate. Commented the Jackson *Clarion Ledger*, "At the time of his death he was canvassing Jasper County as a Republican candidate for the Constitutional Convention, and was daily and nightly denouncing the white people in his speeches and caucuses. . . . Then one or more persons decided that Cook must die. The *Clarion-Ledger* regrets the manner of his killing, as assassination cannot be condoned at any time. Yet the people of Jasper are to be congratulated that they will not be further annoyed by March Cook." (Jackson *Clarion-Ledger*, July 31, 1890, as quoted in Vernon L. Wharton, *The Negro in Mississippi, 1865–1890* (1947), 211.

In another instance, after Hoke Smith's election on a white supremacy campaign in 1906, there were four days of rioting in Atlanta. Fired by newspaper accounts of four assaults on white women by blacks, white mobs engaged in looting and burning black property and attacking blacks. Four blacks were killed and many injured. Franklin, *From Slavery to Freedom*, 323–24; Woodward, *Strange Career*, 86–87.

28. V. O. Key, Jr., major proponent of the *fait accomplit* thesis, states, "Before their formal disfranchisement Negroes had, in most states, ceased to be of much political significance and the whites had won control of state governments." V. O. Key, Jr., *Southern Politics in State and Nation* (1949), 535. J. Morgan Kousser agrees with Key that there was "a stage previous to disfranchisement in which political activity was muted," but credits the disfranchisement laws themselves with effecting a more significant percentage of actual disfranchisement. He claims that the drop in black voting prior to the enactment of disfranchisement provisions in many southern states, brought about through violence, intimidation, fraud, or preliminary legislative restrictions, was relatively small. J. Morgan Kousser, *The Shaping of Southern Politics* (1974), 244. Thus these scholars may be seen to disagree on the more fundamental question of the role of law as it applies to this era. Says Key, "Oddly enough those who urge an institutional change to enable them to gain power usually first win control without benefit of the procedural or organizational advantage they seek. Law often merely records not what is to be but what is, and ensures that what is will continue to be." Key, *Southern Politics*, 535. Kousser, on the other hand, believes that voting restriction was the result of the "*enforcement* not the nonenforcement of the laws." Kousser, *Shaping of Southern Politics* 264. He thus sees legalized disfranchisement as having a far stronger effect than an informal system of voting restriction; through the withdrawal of even symbolic rights, the black person, the poor person and the illiterate person were left demoralized and without hope. Kousser, *Shaping of Southern Politics* 263–64.

29. For discussion of intimidation, violence, fraud, and manipulation of election procedures, see William Mabry, *The Negro in North Carolina Politics since Reconstruction*, Historical Papers of the Trinity College Historical Society, Series XXIII (1940) 67–70; Key, *Southern Politics*, 536, 540; Kousser, *Shaping of Southern Politics*, 14, 45–47, 234–45; Paul Lewinson, *Race Class and Party: A History of Negro Suffrage and White Politics*

in the South (1959), 76–77; Charles Wynes, *Race Relations in Virginia, 1870–1902* (1969), 59–60; Franklin, *From Slavery to Freedom*, 323–24; Woodward, *Strange Career*, 86–87, and Wharton, *The Negro in Mississippi*, 211.

30. J. M. Kousser views this first period of active disfranchisement as coinciding with the threat of the Republican-sponsored Lodge Force Bill. Georgia's poll tax requirement, passed in 1877, predated all other voting restrictions. Between 1889 and 1892, Florida, Mississippi, Tennessee, and Arkansas also adopted a poll tax. During this same period, Tennessee, Mississippi, and Arkansas passed the secret ballot, with Alabama adopting this measure in 1893. Mississippi, the first and only state during this period to call a constitutional convention for the purpose of disfranchisement, added a literacy test and a property clause to the voting restrictions already mentioned. By 1893, South Carolina, Tennessee, and Alabama had enacted registration rules and South Carolina and Florida had adopted multiple-box laws. Kousser, *Shaping of Southern Politics*, 238.

31. See Wharton, *The Negro in Mississippi*, 199–215; Albert Kirwan, *Revolt of the Rednecks, Mississippi Politics: 1876–1925* (1964), 58–64; George Tindall, *South Carolina Negroes, 1877–1900* (1952), 68–91; Joseph Brittain, *Negro Suffrage and Politics in Alabama Since 1870* (1958), 125–70; Wynes, *Race Relations in Virginia, 1870–1902* (1961), 51–67; F. Williams, "The Poll Tax as a Suffrage Requirement in the South, 1870–1901," *Journal of Southern History*, XVIII (1952), 469; and Kousser, *Shaping of Southern Politics*, 139–81.

32. South Carolina in 1894 passed a new registration law to keep blacks from voting prior to its convention. It retained on the voting rolls all those previously registered, most of whom were white, but set up extremely confusing regulations for those not yet registered. In addition, local officials were encouraged to refuse registration blanks to blacks; officials who were unwilling to do so were removed. When a federal district court ruled the registration law unconstitutional, the circuit overturned the decision, stating that the courts lacked jurisdiction over "political questions." Prior to Louisiana's convention in 1898, a secret ballot rule and a new registration law passed in order to insure the election of Democratic delegates to the convention. The secret ballot law prohibited election officials from helping illiterates. The registration law caused more difficulties for illiterates and also permitted two representatives of a political party or a registrar to purge the voting lists for any reason, a purged elector being permitted to file a challenge. The registration act alone cut white registration in half and black registration by 90 percent. In Alabama, although no laws were passed to restrict suffrage prior to its constitutional convention, fraud was clearly indicated (and sometimes publicly admitted) in counties with over 50 percent black residents which voted *for* the calling of the convention and the subsequent ratification of the disfranchising amendments. Kousser, *Shaping of Southern Politics*, 147–71; Tindall, *South Carolina Negroes*, 75–80. For discussion of violence and fraud preceding disfranchising conventions in Virginia and Mississippi, see Wynes, *Race Relations in Virginia*, 59–60, and Wharton, *The Negro in Mississippi*, 211.

33. Although some delegates of the Virginia convention maintained

that it had been called to discuss a wide variety of questions, Charles Wynes concludes that it most probably was called with the main intent of disfranchising blacks. Asked one delegate, A. P. Thom, "If you are not to disfranchise our black men, why are we here?" *Proceedings and Debates of the Constitutional Convention of 1901–1902*, II, 2974, as quoted in Wynes, *Race Relations in Virginia*, 61. The chairman of the Alabama convention said in his opening address that the convention would establish "legal white supremacy without disfranchising a single white man," although he added that many blacks would qualify and be stimulated to learn to read and write. Whether blacks would vote or not may have been a matter of debate, but clearly the convention revolved around questions of the black franchise. *Journal of the Proceedings of the Constitutional Convention of 1901*, 9–12 as quoted in Brittain, *Negro Suffrage*, 129–30. A Mississippi delegate stated, "All understood and desired that some scheme would be evolved which would effectually remove from the sphere of politics in the State the ignorant and unpatriotic negro." Dabney, *Proceedings of the Reunion of the Survivors of the Constitutional Convention of 1890 on the Twentieth Anniversary of the Adoption of the Constitution, held in the Senate Chamber of the Capital at Jackson, Mississippi, November 1st, 1910*, as quoted in Kirwan, *Revolt of the Rednecks*, 66.

34. In Mississippi, South Carolina, and Virginia, the new constitutions were not submitted to the state at large for ratification but were merely promulgated, largely to avoid a political battle and skirt the embarrassing position of asking a good part of the population to vote for their own disfranchisement. The absence of popular ratification was particularly heinous in Virginia where the citizens had originally been encouraged to vote for the calling of the convention on the basis of the fact that they would be able to vote on the new constitution resulting. Wynes, *Race Relations in Virginia*, 64–66. See also Tindall, *South Carolina Negroes*, 88; Wharton, *Negro in Mississippi*, 214.

35. In 1900, North Carolina voters agreed to amendments instituting a poll tax, literacy and property tests. In 1902, Texas voters ratified a poll tax amendment. The literacy test, property test, understanding clause, and grandfather clause were accepted in a Georgia referendum in 1908. In 1889, Florida adopted the poll tax and multiple-box law. In the same year, Tennessee established registration requirements and the secret ballot and added the poll tax a year later. Arkansas passed a secret ballot requirement in 1891 and the poll tax in 1892. Kousser, *Shaping of Southern Politics*, 91–138, 182–223.

36. *Ibid.*, 39.

37. *Ibid.*, 47–56; Key, *Southern Politics*, 536–39; Woodward, *Origins*, 55–56.

38. Kousser, *Shaping of Southern Politics, passim:* Woodward, *Origins*, 321–49; Key, *Southern Politics*, 535–39; Williams, "Poll Tax", 469; Thurgood Marshall, "The Rise and Collapse of the 'White Democratic Primary,'" *Journal of Negro Education*, XXVI (1957), 249.

39. For discussions of southern Democratic reaction to national Republican politics, see Kousser, *Shaping of Southern Politics*, 29–32; Key, *Southern Politics*, 537; Wharton, *Negro in Mississippi*, 208.

40. See Tindall, *South Carolina Negroes*, 73, Lewinson, *Race, Class and Party*, 121; Key, *Southern Politics*, 540–41.

41. Kousser, *Shaping of Southern Politics*, 257–61; Key, *Southern Politics*, 539–41; Wynes, *Race Relations in Virginia*, 56; Wharton, *Negro in Mississippi*, 208; Mabry, *Negro in North Carolina Politics*, 57; Brittain, *Negro Suffrage*, 125; Tindall, *South Carolina Negroes*, 68.

42. Mangum, *Legal Status of the Negro*, 412.

43. See Mabry, *Negro in North Carolina Politics*, 62; Wharton, *Negro in Mississippi*, 208.

44. The leaders of the disfranchisement movements in the southern states generally came from the black belt, were the sons or grandsons of plantation owners, and were generally affluent and well-educated. Kousser, *Shaping of Southern Politics*, 246–50.

45. For a discussion of U.S. imperialism, see Faulkner, *Social Justice*, 29, 308–32; Woodward, *Origins*, 324–26; Logan, *Betrayal of the Negro*, 271–73, and Gossett, *Race*, 310–38.

46. 189 U.S. 475 (1903). For discussion of this case, see Mangum, *Legal Status of the Negro*, 402. See also the Mississippi cases contesting the suffrage provisions of the 1890 constitutional convention. The restrictions were upheld by both the state court in Dixon v. State, 74 Miss. 271 (1896) and Sproule v. Fredericks, 69 Miss. 898 (1892), and by the Supreme Court in Williams v. Mississippi, 170 U.S. 213 (1898). See also Breedlove v. Shuttles, 302 U.S. 277 (1937) in which the Supreme Court ruled that the poll tax did not violate any constitutional rights.

47. 189 U.S. at 488.

48. Guinn v. United States 238 U.S. 437 (1915).

49. During this period, the Supreme Court looked less favorably on the white primary than on other voting restrictions. In Nixon v. Herndon, 273 U.S. 536 (1924) it ruled that a Texas statute forbidding black participation in primaries was unconstitutional. The Court also rejected a change in the statute delegating the State Executive Committee of the Democratic party to fix voting qualifications for the primary in Nixon v. Condon, 286 U.S. 73 (1932). However, in Grovey v. Townsend, 295 U.S. 45 (1935), the Supreme Court upheld the right of the Democratic party to limit its membership by state convention as opposed to Executive Committee because the convention action was not state action but party action, protected as an exercise of private associational rights under the Texas Bill of Rights. In United States v. Classic, 313 U.S. 299 (1941), the Court held that the corrupt acts of election officials in a Louisiana primary were subject to congressional sanctions. In Smith v. Allwright, 321 U.S. 649 (1944), employing the reasoning of *Classic*, the Court concluded that discrimination effected by a state convention, denying blacks the right to participate in primaries, is state action where, in conducting the primary, the party was fulfilling duties delegated to it by the statutory electoral scheme. In Terry v. Adams, 345 U.S. 461 (1953), the Court declared the plaintiffs had the right to vote in a primary held by a private organization, the Jaybird Association, even though the primary was not regulated by state statute. In Rice v. Elmore, 165 F.2d 387 (4th Cir. 1947), *cert. denied*, 333 U.S. 875 (1948) the Court voided the South Carolina white primary and in

Baskin v. Brown, 174 F.2d 391 (4th Cir. 1949) the Court held South Carolina's Democratic primary to violate the Fifteenth Amendment, even though South Carolina had repealed all statutory control of primaries and left them in private hands.

50. Although many industries segregated their employees privately, there were also some statutes prescribing segregation. Arkansas, Oklahoma, Tennessee, and Texas required separate washrooms for blacks and whites in the mining industry. North Carolina called for the maintenance of separate toilets for blacks and whites in manufacturing and other businesses. South Carolina required segregation of employees working in the cotton textile manufacturing industry, with the statute establishing rules of great detail. See Murray, *Laws on Race,* 17–18; Mangum, *Legal Status of the Negro,* 174–75.

51. For a general discussion of blacks in industry, see Charles Wesley, *Negro Labor in the United States, 1850–1925* (1927), and Lorenzo Greene and Carter Woodson, *The Negro Wage Earner* (1930). For discussion focused on the black worker's relationship to the unions, see also Ray Marshall, *The Negro Worker* (1967), 92–93; Sterling Spero and Abram Harris, *The Black Worker* (1931, reprinted 1968); Julius Jacobson, *The Negro and the American Labor Movement,* and William Gould, *Black Workers in White Unions: Job Discrimination in the United States* (1977).

52. After the Civil War, the sale or rental of farmland to blacks was at times prohibited, either through the informal agreements of citizens or by law. See, e.g., Mississippi Session Laws, regular session 82 (1865 in Wharton, *Negro in Mississippi,* 64. Later, mortgage, lien, and other assorted tenancy laws came to protect the interests of landlords over tenants. An 1878 law passed by Democrats in South Carolina entitled landlords to liens on one-third of a crop without recording or filing in a courthouse, and liens of over one-third if filed. Previously, Republicans had forbidden liens over more than one-third of a crop. Tindall, *South Carolina Negroes,* 110. Statutes were also passed permitting verbal labor contracts rather than the witnessed contracts prescribed under Reconstruction legislation. The verbal contracts permitted landlords greater sway. Said Thomas E. Miller of South Carolina in 1891, "In my state if the employer states verbally that the unpaid laborer of his plantation contracted to work for the year no other farmer dares employ the man if he attempts to break the contract rather than work for nothing: for down there it is a misdemeanor to do so, the penalty is heavy, and the farmer who employs the unpaid, starving laborer of his neighbor is the victim of the court." 12 Cong. Rec. 2693 (1891) as quoted in Tindall, *South Carolina Negroes,* 112. The punitive sections of tenancy laws were generally either exclusively directed towards tenants or prescribed heavier penalties for tenants than for landlords. In the North Carolina case of State v. Williams, 32 S.C. 123, 10 S.E. 876 (1890), tenants were found guilty under a statute concerning the removal of crops, though it was with "the intent of storing and preserving the crop for which purpose no adequate means existed on the leased premises." Frenise Logan, *The Negro in North Carolina, 1876–1894* (1964), 79. The South Carolina legislature even tried to use the law to prohibit labor organization. In 1886, when the Knights of Labor proposed to organize black agricultural labor in

the South, the legislature introduced a bill making it a misdemeanor for any organization to interfere in agricultural contracts. The bill, however, was never passed. Tindall, *South Carolina Negroes*, 114.

53. Mangum, *Legal Status of the Negro*, 166; Gunnar Myrdal, *An American Dilemma* (1944), 228, 551, 558, 1344–45.

54. An Alabama statute of this type was invalidated in 1914. United States v. Reynolds, 235 U.S. 133. The Court found the statute conducive to peonage because the terms approved for paying the surety might be more onerous than the sentence to hard labor imposed for the crime itself.

55. Peonage Cases, 123 F. 671 (1903).

56. 83 U.S. (16 Wall.) 36 (1873).

57. Bailey v. State, 158 Ala. 18, 48 So. 498 (1908); Townsend v. State, 124 Ga. 69, 52 S.E. 293 (1905). See Mangum, *Legal Status of the Negro*, 167.

58. 219 U.S. 219 (1911). Joined by one other member of the Court, Justice Holmes dissented on the ground that a state was not forbidden by this amendment from punishing a breach of contract as a crime. "Compulsory work for no private master in a jail is not peonage." *Ibid.*, 247.

59. *Ibid.*, 244.

60. Wilson v. State, 138 Ga. 489, 75 S.E. 619 (1912); Phillips v. Bell, 84 Fla. 225, 94 So. 699 (1922); Mangum, *Legal Status of the Negro*, 168.

61. Pollock v. Williams, 322 U.S. 4 (1944); Taylor v. Georgia, 315 U.S. 24 (1942).

62. 109 U.S. 3 (1883).

63. 95 U.S. 485 (1877).

64. 163 U.S. 537 (1896).

65. Laws of Tennessee (1881), 211–12. See Gilbert Stephenson, *Race Distinctions in American Law* (1910, reprinted 1969), 216, and Franklin Johnson, *The Development of State Legislation Concerning the Free Negro* (1919), 16.

66. In 1887, Florida passed a separate coach law purported to be for the protection of blacks. Between 1887 and 1894, Louisiana, Alabama, Arkansas, Georgia, Kentucky, and Texas passed separate coach laws. Stephenson, *Race Distinctions*, 216–17, and Johnson, *The Development of State Legislation*, 14–18.

67. Georgia's separate coach law passed in 1891 was the first to include electrical and street cars. Electrical and street car segregation laws were then adopted by North Carolina and Virginia in 1901, Louisiana in 1902, Arkansas, South Carolina, and Texas in 1903, Mississippi and Maryland in 1904, Florida in 1905, and Oklahoma in 1907. Johnson, *The Development of State Legislation*, 17–18. The above laws prescribed segregation within cars, but Montgomery, in 1906, passed an ordinance calling for a completely separate car for blacks. Woodward, *Strange Career*, 97. For discussion of segregation in boats, steamships, and waiting rooms, see Stephenson, *Race Distinctions*, 214–16, 220–21, and Johnson, *The Development of State Legislation*, 19.

In the 1930s nine states adopted special laws requiring separation of the races on motor carriers, some including requirements for separate waiting rooms in bus stations. According to one author, segregation of motor carriers was practiced in all the southern states whether or not a statute was on the books. Mangum, *Legal Status of the Negro*, 217.

68. Mississippi and South Carolina provided for segregation in hospitals. Thirteen states required the separation of mental patients and seven states made accommodations for black and white tubercular patients. In Alabama white female nurses were not permitted to work in hospitals treating black patients. The states provided for the segregation of prisoners in penal institutions, six of which also stipulated that blacks and whites could not be chained together. Alabama and West Virginia provided for segregation in paupers' homes. Delaware, Louisiana, and West Virginia required segregation of homes for the aged. Seven states provided segregated housing for orphans. Murray, *Laws on Race*, 17.

The races were also separated in amusements and sports. The first such law was the Separate Park Law adopted in 1905 by Georgia. Entrances, exits, ticket sellers and ticket windows were also segregated in circuses by a Louisiana law of 1914. Woodward, *Strange Career*, 99–100.

Residential segregation also developed during this period in a variety of forms. Some laws divided areas into black and white districts and prohibited either race from living in the other's district. Sometimes blocks were designated black or white on the basis of the majority of residents living there and then people of the other race were forbidden to move in. Other laws required people of either race to secure the consent of the majority of persons living in an area before moving in. Much residential segregation was of course effected without statute. Woodward, *Strange Career*, 100–101. The Supreme Court's 1917 decision in Buchanan v. Warley, 245 U.S. 60, striking down a city ordinance that excluded blacks from predominantly white blocks and vice versa, failed to discourage enactment of Jim Crow housing laws.

69. Gong Lum v. Rice, 275 U.S. 78 (1927) (public school); Berea College v. Kentucky, 211 U.S. 45 (1908) (private college); Cumming v. Bd. of Educ., 175 U.S. 528 (1899) (closing of black high school).

70. The absence or gross underrepresentation of blacks on juries can in part be traced to suffrage restrictions which kept blacks off the voter rolls from which jurors were often chosen. See Stephenson, *Race Distinctions*, 247. Moreover, during the period of disfranchisement, judgeships as well as election offices were often changed from elective to appointive positions, permitting the Democrats greater direct control in local affairs. Generally, a greater percentage of blacks than of whites were sentenced to death and, of those condemned, a greater percentage of blacks than of whites were executed. For a general discussion of the court systems, jury selection, and sentences and punishments, see Myrdal, *American Dilemma*, 547–57 and Mangum, *Legal Status of the Negro*, 308–70.

71. In some states, there were heavier penalties for fornication and adultery between whites and blacks than between members of the same race. See Stephenson, *Race Distinctions*, 273–77, and Mangum, *Legal Status of the Negro*, 365–67. For more general discussion, see Joel Kovel, *White Racism: A Psychohistory* (1970); Calvin Hernton, *Sex and Racism in America* (1966); Roger Daniels and Harry Kitano, *American Racism: Explora-*

tion of the Nature of Prejudice (1970); Applebaum, "Miscegenation Statutes: A Constitutional and Social Problem," *Geo. L.J.* LIII (1964), 49.

72. Pace v. Alabama, 106 U.S. 583 (1883).

73. McLaughlin v. Florida, 379 U.S. 184 (1964) and Loving v. Virginia,
388 U.S. 1 (1967).

74. It took fifty years for southern courts to begin to act on the basis of
the opinion in Neal v. Delaware 103 U.S. 370 (1880) in which the Court
seemed to state that prolonged absence of blacks from juries in a particular locale was *prima facie* evidence of discrimination. In 1932, in Lee v.
State, 163 Md. 56, 161 Atl. 284 (1932), a black defendant won a reversal
for demonstrating there had been a long period of time in which blacks had
not sat on juries and that the judge selecting jurors had started with a collection of only the names of eligible white men. Mangum, *Legal Status of
the Negro*, 320–22.

75. As the twentieth century progressed, courts became more willing to
rule out prejudicial language in a trial. E.g. in Cooper v. State 186 So. 23
(Fla. 1939), language calculated to arouse prejudice at a murder trial was
declared to constitute reversible error. In Harris v. State, 96 Miss. 379, 50
So. 626 (1909), language indicating the probability of mob violence if the
jury failed to convict a black for the murder of a white man was declared
reversible error. Cases have also recognized the right to challenge jurors on
grounds of race prejudice. See Pinder v. State, 27 Fla. 370, 8 So. 837
(1891); Hill v. State, 112 Miss. 260, 72 So. 1003 (1916). Other cases have
considered criteria for determination of the race prejudice of jurors. E.g.
Lee v. State, 164 Md. 550, 165 Atl. 614 (1933) (a white juror who does
not consider a black his social equal is not incompetent to serve); State v.
Sanders, 103 S.C. 216, 88 S.E. 10 (1916) (a juror is incompetent who testi-
fies he opposes a black lawyer testifying before a white jury). See Mangum,
Legal Status of the Negro, 274–307, 356–63.

76. Strauder v. West Virginia, 100 U.S. 303 (1880) (state statute held
void which qualified only whites for jury service); Ex parte Virginia, 100
U.S. 339 (1880) (purposeful denial to blacks of right to sit on juries).

77. Powell v. Alabama, 287 U.S. 45 (1932) and Norris v. Alabama, 294
U.S. 587 (1935).

78. See, e.g., *Report of the National Advisory Commission on Civil Dis-
orders* (1967).

79. See, e.g., Washington v. Davis, 426 U.S. 22 (1976), and Village of
Arlington Heights v. Metropolitan Housing Development Corp., 97 S.Ct.
555 (1977), indicating that, in the fields of employment and housing re-
spectively, it is not enough to show that a challenged policy on law has a
disproportionate impact on minorities. Rather, proof of racially discriminatory intent or purpose is required to show a violation of the Constitution. In
Austin Indept. School Dist. v. United States, 97 S.Ct. 517 (1976), this
standard was applied to school desegregation cases.

80. Job seniority: International Brotherhood of Teamsters v. United
States, 97 S.Ct. 1843 (1977); zoning: Village of Arlington Heights v. Metro-
politan Housing Development Corp., *supra* note 90; City of Eastlake v.
Forest City Enterprises, Inc., 426 U.S. 668 (1976); James v. Valtierra, 402

U.S. 137 (1971); neighborhood school assignment: Dayton Bd. of Educ. v. Brinkman, 97 S.Ct. 2776 (1977), election procedures: Whitcomb v. Chavis, 403 U.S. 124 (1971); *cf.* White v. Regester, 412 U.S. 755 (1973).

81. Robert Fogel & Stanley Engerman, *Time on the Cross: The Economics of American Negro Slavery* (1974), 260–61. Citing tentative evidence indicating that life expectancy of blacks declined, the quality of diet and health deteriorated, while job opportunities almost disappeared, the authors suggest that "the attack on the material conditions of blacks after the Civil War was not only more ferocious, but, in certain respects, more cruel than that which preceded it."

82. The motivations of contemporary social scientists are examined in substantial detail in comments on Nathan Glazer's 1975 work, *Affirmative Discrimination: Ethnic Inequality and Public Policy.* See Bell, Book Review, Emory, L. J., XXV (1976), 879.

83. Psychologist Kenneth Clark, in commenting at some length on this phenomenon in an article on "Moral Choices," Miami *Herald,* September 18, 1977, Sec. E, p. 6, writes, "The frequency with which individuals are required to adjust to various forms of moral duplicities in complex societies suggests that apparent acceptance of these inconsistencies is an index of socialization and maturity. . . . These moral conflicts have their personal and social consequences. Individuals are required to cope with them by one or more devices."

84. Alex Haley, *Roots* (1976). One reviewer who admired Haley's novel was far less impressed with the ABC televised version shown over eight straight nights in January, 1977, to an estimated 130 million viewers. She wrote: "Truth, after all, is what actually happened; history is a step away from Truth; Haley's novel is a step away from that; and the televised version is so far away that the *real* people, who suffered beyond imagination, would not recognize their lives. . . . Haley himself has said that history is written by the winners. So, unfortunately, is television." E. Collier, Film Review, *First World* (March–April, 1977), 40–41.

Notes to THE BLACK SOUTHERNER'S RESPONSE TO THE SOUTHERN SYSTEM OF RACE RELATIONS
by Al-Tony Gilmore

1. C. Vann Woodward, *The Strange Career of Jim Crow* (New York: Oxford University Press, 1955), 98.

2. W. E. B. Du Bois, *The Souls of Black Folk* (Greenwich, Conn.: Fawcett Publications, 1961), v.

3. C. Eric Lincoln, *The Black Muslims in America* (Boston: Beacon Press, 1973), 35.

4. Richard M. Dorson, *American Negro Folktales* (Greenwich, Conn.: Fawcett Publications, 1967).

5. Lawrence W. Levine, *Black Culture and Black Consciousness: Afro-American Folk Thought from Slavery to Freedom* (New York: Oxford University Press, 1977), 321–44.

6. John H. Burma, "Humor as a Technique in Race Conflict," *American Sociological Review,* II (1946), 713.

7. *Ibid.*, 712.

8. Benjamin J. Davis, *Communist Councilman From Harlem* (New York: International Publishers, 1969), 22.

9. Al-Tony Gilmore, *Bad Nigger! The National Impact of Jack Johnson* (Port Washington, N.Y.: Kennikat Press, 1975), 9–24.

10. *Ibid.*, 21.

11. Ernest J. Gaines, *The Autobiography of Miss Jane Pittman* (New York: Dial Press, 1971), 201.

12. Maya Angelou, *I Know Why The Caged Bird Sings* (New York: Random House, 1969), 111–15.

13. J. Mason Brewer, *American Negro Folklore* (Chicago: Quadrangle Books, 1972), 44.

14. Levine's *Black Culture and Black Consciousness* contains the most cogent discussion of the role of folklore heroes in Afro-American life and thought.

15. Gunnar Myrdal, *The American Dilemma* (New York: Harper and Row, 1944), I.

16. August Meier and Elliott Rudwick, "Black Violence in the 20th Century: A Study in Rhetoric and Retaliation," in Hugh Davis Graham and Ted Robert Gurr (eds.), *Violence in America* (New York: New American Library, 1969), 380–92; Meier and Rudwick, *From Plantation to Ghetto: An Interpretive History of American Negroes* (New York: Hill and Wing, 1966), 251.

17. Arnold Taylor, *Travail and Triumph, Black Life and Culture in the South Since the Civil War* (Westport, Conn.: Greenwood Press, 1976), 63.

18. William Ivy Hair, *Carnival of Fury, Robert Charles and the New Orleans Race Riot of 1900* (Baton Rouge: Louisiana State University Press, 1976), 178–79.

19. Asa Gordon, *Sketches of Negro Life in South Carolina* (Columbia: University of South Carolina Press, 1975).

20. Dorson, *American Negro Folktales*, 319–20.

21. By far, the most detailed account of Washington's career and his impact on both black and white Americans is Louis Harlan's biographical study, *Booker T. Washington, The Making of a Leader* (New York: Oxford University Press, 1973), I.

22. Walter B. Weare, *Black Business in the New South, A Social History of the North Carolina Mutual Life Insurance Company* (Urbana: University of Illinois Press, 1973).

23. Dorson, *American Negro Folktales*, 309.

24. Amy Jacques Garvey, *Garvey and Garveyism* (New York: MacMillan Company, 1970), 130, 166–67.

25. Dorson, *American Negro Folktales*, 309.

26. Richard Kluger, *Simple Justice, A History of Brown vs. Board of Education* (New York: Random House, 1977).

27. Wilson Record, *The Negro and the Communist Party* (New York: Atheneum, 1971).

28. Theodore Kornweibel, Jr., *No Crystal Stair, Black Life and the Messenger, 1917–1928* (Westport: Greenwood Press, 1975), 225–27. The

best discussion on this subject is Eric Foner, *American Socialism and Black Americans* (Westport: Greenwood Press, 1977).

29. Edwin S. Redkey, *Black Exodus, Black Nationalist and Back-to-Africa Movements, 1890–1910* (New Haven: Yale University Press, 1969), 253–54.

30. Gilbert Geis, *The Longest Way Home: Chief Alfred Sam's Back to Africa Movement* (Detroit: Wayne State University Press, 1964).

Notes to SOUTHERN POLITICAL STYLE
by Dan Carter

1. Ralph McGill, "Civil Rights for the Negro," *Atlantic*, November, 1949, pp. 64–66.

2. Estimates of Negro voting on some cases amounts to "guestimates," but the most reliable figures seem to be those furnished by Luther P. Jackson in "Race and Suffrage in the South Since 1040," *New South*, III (June–July, 1948), 3. The NAACP released figures which were considerably higher, but these have been challenged by other scholars. See V. O. Key, *Southern Politics in State and Nation* (New York: Random House, 1949), 522.

3. Samuel Lubell, *The Future of American Politics* (New York: Harper and Row, 1952), 106–107; Hugh Douglas Price, *The Negro and Southern Politics: A Chapter of Florida History* (New York: New York University Press, 1957), 60–61, 119; Richard Fried, *Men Against McCarthy* (New York: Columbia University Press, 1976), 98–101; Ralph McGill, "Can He Purge Senator Pepper," *Saturday Evening Post*, April 22, 1950, pp. 32–33, 141–43.

4. Hugh Douglas Price, "The Negro and Florida Politics, 1944–1954," *Journal of Politics*, XVII (May, 1955), 198–220; Robert Sherrill, *Gothic Politics in the Deep South* (New York: Grossman Publishers, 1968), 136–73.

5. Lubell, *The Future of American Politics*, 110; Fried, *Men Against McCarthy*, 98–101; New York *Times*, June 25, 26, 1950.

6. Sherrill, *Gothic Politics*, 241–46; *Nation*, July 24, 1950, p. 69; *New Republic*, July 24, 1950, p. 7; New York *Times*, June 18, 1950. The sympathetic biographers of Thurmond and Johnston make only brief and apologetic references to the 1950 campaign. See John Erwin Huss, *Senator for the South: A Biography of Olin D. Johnston* (New York: Doubleday, 1961), and Alberta Lachicutte, *Rebel Senator: Strom Thurmond* (New York: Devin Adair, Inc., 1966).

7. C. Vann Woodward, *Origins of the New South* (Baton Rouge: Louisiana State University Press, 1949), 348–54.

8. Albert D. Kirwan, *Revolt of the Rednecks: Mississippi Politics, 1876–1925* (Lexington: University of Kentucky Press, 1951), 10. For a useful review of some aspects of the racial politics of Mississippi during this period, see Willie D. Halsell's "James R. Chalmers and Mahoneism in Mississippi," *Journal of Southern History*, X (February, 1944), 37–58, and her edited article "Republican Factionalism in Mississippi, 1882–1884," *Journal of Southern History*, VII (February, 1941), 84–101. Also useful is John R. Lynch, *Reminiscences of an Active Life: The Autobiography of John Roy*

Lynch, edited with an introduction by John Hope Franklin (Chicago: University of Chicago Press, 1970), 255–300, 333–48.

9. William Cooper, *The Conservative Regime: South Carolina, 1877–1890* (Baltimore: Johns Hopkins University Press, 1968), 92–93.

10. J. Morgan Kousser, *The Shaping of Southern Politics: Suffrage Restriction and the Establishment of the One-Party South, 1880–1910* (New Haven: Yale University Press, 1974). Kousser's extensive bibliography on interracial politics in the South in the critical years after Reconstruction reflects the significant work that has been done in this area and includes the groundbreaking monographs of Albert Kirwan, Vernon Lane Wharton, Helen Edmonds, and George Tindall, as well as the newer works by William J. Cooper on South Carolina; Allen J. Going, William Rogers, and Sheldon Hackney on Alabama: William Ivy Hair on Louisiana: Olive Hall Shadgett on Georgia; Jack P. Maddex, Allen W. Moger, Raymond H. Pulley, and Charles E. Wynes on Virginia, and Lawrence D. Rice on Texas. Since the publication of Kousser's book, there have been two relevant studies of Tennessee, Roger L. Hart's *Redeemer, Bourbons and Populists, Tennessee, 1870–1896* (Baton Rouge: Louisiana State University Press, 1975), and Joseph H. Cartwright's *The Triumph of Jim Crow: Tennessee Race Relations in the 1880's* (Knoxville: University of Tennessee Press, 1976).

11. For a brief look at the history of the "Open Letter Club" see Mort Sosna's *In Search of the Silent South: Southern Liberals and the Race Issue* (New York: Columbia University Press, 1977), 4–9.

12. William Alexander Percy, *Lanterns on the Levee* (New York: Alfred A. Knopf, 1941), 148–49.

·13. Allan A. Michie and Frank Rhylick, *Dixie Demagogues* (New York: Vanguard Press, 1969), 265–66. For a less flamboyant, but far more useful survey of the career of "Cotton Ed," see Selden Kennedy Smith's "Ellison Durant Smith: A Southern Progressive, 1909–1929" (Ph.D. dissertation, University of South Carolina, 1970).

14. There are several versions of this example of Vardaman's invective. This is the original quotation from his newspaper, the Greenwood (Miss.) *Commonwealth,* May 26, 1898, in which Vardaman attacked a journalistic opponent, Charles E. Wright of the Vicksburg *Dispatch.*

15. Under these circumstances, it is not surprising that Sullens suggested a replacement of the capitol dome's great golden eagle with a "puking buzzard," should Bilbo be elected in 1915. Jackson *Daily News,* February 23, May 16, 1915. Although the golden eagle remained in place after Bilbo's election, opponents later presented Bilbo with a stuffed buzzard which was placed in the "educational exhibits" of the Agriculture Department at the state capitol.

16. Bobby Wade Saucier, "The Public Career of Theodore G. Bilbo" (Ph.D. dissertation, Tulane University, 1971), 71.

17. The notion of Reconstruction as "barbarism run amok" is one of the most important myths of southern history. For some reflections on the power and political utility of this mythology see Dan T. Carter, "The Forgotten Centennial" (Atlanta: Emory University Publications, 1976).

18. For an account of the Indianola episode, see Willard B. Gatewood's "Theodore Roosevelt and the Indianola Affair," *Journal of Negro History,*

LIII (January, 1968), 48–69. Louis Harlan discusses the reaction to the Roosevelt-Washington dinner in *Booker T. Washington* (New York: Oxford University Press, 1972), 311–24.

19. William F. Holmes, *The Great White Chief: James Kimble Vardaman* (Baton Rouge: Louisiana State University Press, 1970), 105; *The Outlook,* September 12, 1903, p. 139.

20. For an excellent recent biography of Talmadge see William Anderson's *The Wild Man from Sugar Creek: The Political Career of Eugene Talmadge* (Baton Rouge: Louisiana State University Press, 1975).

21. Percy, *Lanterns on the Levee,* 148–49.

22. Raymond Gram Swing, *Forerunners of American Fascism* (New York: Julian Messner, Inc., 1935); Michie and Rhylick, *Dixie Demagogues;* Hilton Butler, "Bilbo—the Two-edged Sword: A Mussolini for our Most Backward State," *North American Review,* December, 1931, pp. 496–593; Louis Cochran, "Mussolini of Mississippi," *The Outlook,* June 17, 1931, pp. 203–205. Nor were such observations restricted to the 1930s. See Victor C. Ferkiss, "The Political and Economic Philosophy of American Fascism" (Ph.D. dissertation, University of Chicago, 1954).

23. Clement Eaton sensitively described the nature of this class tension in his essay "The Southern Yeoman: The Humorists' View and the Reality" in Eaton's *The Mind of the Old South* (rev. ed.; Baton Rouge: Louisiana State University Press, 1967).

24. T. Harry Williams, *Huey Long* (New York: Alfred A. Knopf, 1969), especially pp. 737–847.

25. Tindall's essay which originally appeared in *Virginia Quarterly* has been reprinted in his recent collection *The Ethnic Southerner* (Baton Rouge: Louisiana State University Press, 1976), 163–84.

26. Reinhard H. Luthin, *American Demagogues: Twentieth Century* (Boston: Beacon Press, 1954).

27. Bilbo claimed that "dago" was "only slang" for Italian. He also denied he had made a reference to "every damn Jew from Jesus Christ on down," only to be confronted with affidavits from several members of the audience. See "Dear Dago," *Commonweal,* XLII (October, 1945), 396–97; "Prince of the Peckerwoods," *Time,* July 1, 1946, pp. 22–23; Saucier, "Public Career of Bilbo," 240. Vardaman supported the Supreme Court nomination of Louis Brandeis and, according to his biographer, used anti-Catholic rhetoric only once in his political career. Holmes, *The Great White Chief,* 366.

28. Williams, *Huey Long,* 414–15. For a discussion of the origins of the term, see Joseph Lincoln Steffens, *The Autobiography of Lincoln Steffens* (New York: Harcourt, Brace and Company, 1931), 374.

29. James W. Garner, "A Mississippian on Vardaman," *The Outlook,* September 5, 1903, pp. 1–2. It was a theme to which Garner later returned after he was named professor of political science at the University of Illinois. In a remarkably candid essay, "Southern Politics Since the Civil War," which he wrote in 1914, Garner made clear what was implicit in his earlier letter. White Mississippians differed only in their estimate of the political danger posed by black Mississippians. They were "rightfully" united in their view that the maintenance of white supremacy was essential

in order to prevent "the very existence of their civilization." See John A. Fairlie (ed.), *Studies in Government and International Law by James Wilford Garner* (Urbana: University of Illinois Press, 1943), 76–91. For a description of the extraordinary eruption of racial viciousness in the 1903 Mississippi campaign see Eugene E. White's "Anti-Racial Agitation in Politics: James Kimble Vardaman in the Mississippi Gubernatorial Campaign of 1903," *Journal of Mississippi History*, VII (April, 1945), 91–110.

30. Robert Wiebe, *The Segmented Society: An Introduction to the Meanings of America* (New York: Oxford University Press, 1975), 77.

31. This is not meant to imply that the various social scientists and historians of modernization have directly argued that legal segregation is incompatible with the process of modernization. I would simply suggest that the presence of such a glaring social and legal contradiction of the values of modernization raises questions about the utility of this concept in measuring social change. The literature of "modernization" is vast and complex. John Brode (ed.), *The Process of Modernization—An Annotated Bibliography* (Cambridge, Mass.: Harvard University Press, 1969), summarizes the literature published before 1969. More recently Richard D. Brown and Raimondo Luraghi have made a number of general observations concerning North-South differences. See Luraghi's "The Civil War and the Modernization of American Society: Social Structure and Industrial Revolution in the Old South before and during the War," *Civil War History*, XVIII (September, 1972), 230–50, and Brown's "Modernization: A Victorian Climax," *American Quarterly*, XXVII (December, 1975), 533–48.

32. Ben J. Wattenberg (ed.), *The Statistical History of the United States from Colonial Times to the Present* (New York: Basic Books, Inc., 1976), 22, 459; *United States Census of Manufactures, 1954* (Washington: Government Printing Office, 1954), III, 10–56; Ransom and Sutch, *One Kind of Freedom: The Economic Consequences of Emancipation* (Cambridge, England, and New York: Cambridge University Press, 1977). For an indispensable survey of the recent literature on economic developments in the New South, see Harold Woodman's "Sequel to Slavery: The New History Views of the Postbellum South," *Journal of Southern History* (November, 1977), 523–54. Blaine Brownell views the development of several southern cities in the 1920s from one perspective in *The Urban Ethos in the South, 1920–1930* (Baton Rouge: Louisiana State University Press, 1975). For an overview of the modern urban South, see Blaine Brownell and David Goldfield (eds.), *The City in Southern History: The Growth of Urban Civilization in the South* (Port Washington, N.J.: Kennikat Press, 1977).

33. William D. Miller, *Mr. Crump of Memphis* (Baton Rouge: Louisiana State University Press, 1964), 102–103, 121; Cartwright, *The Triumph of Jim Crow*, 140–46. In Chattanooga, blacks served on the city council as late as 1910, but these were to be the last black politicians to serve in such an office in a major southern city for half a century. Brownell and Goldfield, *The City in Southern History*, 153.

34. Shields McIlwaine, *Memphis, Down in Dixie* (New York: E. P. Dutton and Company, Inc., 1948), 375; Memphis *Commercial Appeal*, August 5, 1914.

150 Notes

35. McIlwaine, *Memphis,* 319–23; Clarence L. Kelley, "Robert R. Church, a Negro Tennessean in Republican State and National Politics from 1912–1932" (M.A. thesis, Tennessee A.&I., 1954). More recently, descendants of Church have assembled an adulatory biography which—despite its limitations—contains considerable valuable primary materials on the role of Church in the politics of Memphis and Tennessee. Annettee E. Church and Roberta Church, *The Robert R. Churches of Memphis: A Father and Son Who Achieved in Spite of Race* (Ann Arbor, Mich.: 1974).

36. David M. Tucker, *Lieutenant Lee of Beale Street* (Nashville: Vanderbilt University Press, 1971); George W. Lee, "The Political Upheaval in Memphis," *The Messenger,* (February, 1928), 30–31.

37. McIlwaine, *Memphis,* 319; Lee, "The Political Upheaval in Memphis," 30. Paul Lewinson gives a brief description of the extent of black participation in Memphis politics in *Race, Class and Party* (London: Oxford University Press, 1932), 138–41.

38. William Fleming, "San Antonio: The History of a Military City, 1865–1880" (Ph.D. dissertation, University of Pennsylvania, 1964), 21–33, 69, 135–37.

39. Green Payton, *San Antonio* (New York: McGraw Hill, 1946); Ralph J. Bunche, *The Political Status of the Negro in the Age of FDR* (Chicago: University of Chicago Press, 1973), 464–65. There is no account of twentieth-century politics in San Antonio comparable to the works by Miller and Tucker on Memphis. William Fleming's study is excellent, but it treats only the years from 1865 to 1880. The best source for a history of the Bellinger machine would undoubtedly be the files of the San Antonio *Register.* This black newspaper has been published by the Bellinger family since the early 1930s, but back files are available only in the *Register* office and neither the present editor nor owner would respond to requests for permission to examine the newspaper.

40. Quoted in Mary Maverick, *A Maverick American* (New York: Covici, Friede Publishers, 1937), 133.

41. Velmo Bellinger is still listed as the owner and publisher of the *Register.*

42. Any study of the Bellinger "machine" will have to unravel the relationships between Bellinger and the black and tan faction which supported Republican Congressman Harry M. Wurzback in the early 1930s. At the same time that Bellinger backed Wurzback, he maintained close ties with nominally Democratic leaders in San Antonio. For a survey of San Antonio in the 1930s which unfortunately neglects interracial politics, see Mary Maverick McMillan Fisher's "San Antonio," in Robert C. Cotner, *et al., Texas Cities and the Great Depression* (Austin: Texas Memorial Museum, 1973), 53–90.

43. Owen P. White, "Machine Made," *Colliers,* September 18, 1937, p. 32.

44. Bunche, *The Political Status of the Negro,* 464–65; Payton, *San Antonio,* 190–91. During the middle of the depression, for example, the welfare rights of San Antonio blacks seem to have been protected more than in other southern cities. See Cotner, *Texas Cities,* 87.

45. Miller, *Mr. Crump,* 28–31; Payton, *San Antonio,* 178–79.
46. George M. Reynolds, *Machine Politics in New Orleans, 1897–1926* (New York: Columbia University Press, 1936), 77–78, 224–39; Joy Jackson, *New Orleans in the Gilded Age: Politics and Urban Progress, 1880–1889* (Baton Rouge: Louisiana State University Press, 1969), 33–34, 315–18; Edward F. Haas, *DeLesseps S. Morrison and the Image of Reform: New Orleans Politics, 1946–1961* (Baton Rouge: Louisiana State University Press, 1974), 67–81; Clarence A. Bacote, "The Negro in Atlanta Politics," *Phylon* (Fourth Quarter, 1955), 331–50.
47. Walter B. Weare, *Black Business in the New South: A Social History of the North Carolina Mutual Life Insurance Company* (Urbana: University of Illinois Press, 1973), 212–14.

Notes to REPRESSION OF BLACKS IN THE SOUTH, 1890–1945
by Mary Frances Berry

1. C. Vann Woodward, *The Strange Career of Jim Crow* (New York, 1974); George B. Tindall, *South Carolina Negroes; 1877–1900* (Columbia, S.C., 1952); Frenise A. Logan, The *Negro in North Carolina 1876–1894* (Chapel Hill, 1964); John W. Blassingame, *Black New Orleans 1860–1880* (Chicago, 1973); Dale Somers, "Black and White in New Orleans; A Study in Urban Race Relations, 1865–1900," *Journal of Southern History,* XL (February, 1974), 19–42; Joel Williamson, *After Slavery; The Negro in South Carolina During Reconstruction, 1861–1877* (Chapel Hill, 1965); Vernon Lane Wharton, *The Negro in Mississippi, 1865–1890* (Chapel Hill, 1947); Roger Fischer, *The Segregation Struggle in Louisiana, 1862–77* (Urbana, Ill., 1974).
2. James T. Moore, "Black Militancy in Readjuster, Virginia 1879–83," *Journal of Southern History,* XLI (May, 1975), 167–88, Thomas Holt, *Black Over White: Negro Political Leadership in South Carolina During Reconstruction* (Urbana, Ill., 1977); Charles R. Vincent, *Black Legislators in Louisiana During Reconstruction* (Baton Rouge, 1976); John Hope Franklin, "Legal Disfranchisement of the Negro," *Journal of Negro Education,* XXVI (Spring, 1957), 241–48; Allen W. Trelease, *White Terror: The Ku Klux Klan Conspiracy and Southern Reconstruction* (New York, 1971); Mary Frances Berry, *Black Resistance/White Law, A History of Constitutional Racism in America* (Englewood Cliffs, N.J., 1971 [4]), 103–19; Clarence Bacote, "Negro Proscriptions, Protests; and Proposed Solutions in Georgia; 1880–1908," *The Journal of Southern History,* XXV (November, 1959) 47–98. David M. Chalmers, *Hooded America, The First Century of the Ku Klux Klan* (New York, 1965).
3. Mary Frances Berry, *Military Necessity and Civil Rights Policy, Black Citizenship and the Constitution, 1861–1868* (Port Washington, N.Y., 1977); Otis Singletary, *The Negro Militia and Reconstruction* (Austin, Tex., 1957); Howard N. Rabinowitz, "From Exclusion to Segregation, 'Southern Race Relations,' 1865–1890," *Journal of American History,* LXIII (September, 1976), 325–33, and notes there cited; Leon Litwack, *North of Slavery, The Negro In the Free States 1790–1860* (Chicago, 1961).

4. Rabinowitz, "From Exclusion to Segregation," 343–45.

5. *Ibid*, 347–48; W. R. Hogan and E. A. Davis (eds.), *William Johnson's Natchez: The Ante-Bellum Diary of a Free Negro* (Baton Rouge, 1951); Franklin, "Legal Disfranchisement of the Negro," 241–48.

6. Berry, *Black Resistance/White Law*, Chapters 8–10; Loren Miller, *The Petitioners: The Story of the Supreme Court of the United States and the Negro* (New York, 1966), 2–3; David W. Bishop, "The Attitude of the Interstate Commerce Commission Towards Discrimination on Public Carriers, 1889–1910" (M.A. thesis, Howard University).

7. Gordon C. Lee, *The Struggle for Federal Aid; First Phase A History of the Attempts To Obtain Federal Aid for the Common Schools, 1870–1890* (New York, 1949), 7; Daniel W. Crofts, "The Black Response to the Blair Education Bill," *Journal of Southern History*, XXXVII (February, 1971), 41–65; Rayford W. Logan, *The Betrayal of the Negro from Rutherford B. Hayes to Woodrow Wilson* (New York, 1965), 70–82, 197.

8. Franklin, "Legal Disfranchisement of the Negro," 241–48; Vincent DeSantis, *Republicans Face the Southern Question, 1877–1897* (Baltimore, 1959); Stanley P. Hirshon, *Farewell to the Bloody Shirt: Northern Republicans and the Southern Negro, 1877–1893* (Bloomington, Ind., 1962).

9. Holt, *Black Over White*, 208–24; Vincent, *Black Legislators in Louisiana;* Okon Edet Uya, *From Slavery to Public Service: Robert Smalls, 1839–1915* (New York, 1971), 127–29.

10. William F. Holmes, "The Demise of the Colored Farmers Alliance," *Journal of Southern History*, XLI (May, 1975), 187–200; William I. Hair, *Bourbonism and Agrarian Protest Louisiana Politics, 1877–1900,* (Baton Rouge, 1969).

11. Rabinowitz, "From Exclusion to Segregation," 348–50; Litwack, *North of Slavery;* Forrest G. Wood, *Black Scare: The Racist Response to Emancipation and Reconstruction* (Berkeley, 1968); V. Jacque Voegeli, *Free, But Not Equal: The Midwest and The Negro During the Civil War* (Chicago, 1967).

12. Guion Griffis Johnson, "Southern Paternalism Toward Negroes After Emancipation," *Journal of Southern History*, XXIII (November, 1957), 483–509.

13. Logan, *Betrayal of the Negro*, 22, 242–75, 371–92; Loften Mitchell, *Black Drama, The Story of the American Negro in the Theatre* (New York, 1967), 33, 38–39; Frederick W. Bond, *The Negro and the Drama* (College Park, Md., 1940).

14. Sterling A. Brown, *The Negro in American Fiction* (Washington, 1937); Francis P. Gaines, *The Southern Plantation; A Study in the Development and Accuracy of a Tradition* (New York, 1924); Margaret Just Butcher, *The Negro in American Culture* (New York, 1956), 58–60; Otto H. Olsen, *Carpetbagger's Crusade: The Life of Albion Winegar Tourgee* (Baltimore, 1963); Louis D. Rubin, Jr., *George W. Cable: The Life and Times of a Southern Heretic* (New York, 1969), Chapters 18–23.

15. Robert Toll, *Blacking Up The Minstrel Show in Nineteenth Century America* (New York, 1974) 161, 195–229, 245.

16. Donald Bogle, *Toms, Coons, Mulattoes, Mammies and Bucks, An Interpretive History of Blacks in American Films* (New York, 1973), 2–3;

Edith J. R. Isaacs, *The Negro in the American Theatre* (New York, 1947), 39.

17. John R. Commons, *Races and Immigrants in America* (New York, 1915), 7. Bert J. Lowenberg, "The Reaction of American Scientists to Darwinism," *American Historical Review* XXXVIII (1933), 687.

18. Logan, *Betrayal of the Negro*, 172–73; 271–72, Richard Hofstadter, *Social Darwinism in American Thought* (Philadelphia, 1945), 146; Josiah Strong, *Our Country: Its Possible Future and Its Present Crisis* (New York, 1885), 175–78.

19. Lothrop Stoddard, *The Rising Tide of Color Against White Supremacy* (New York, 1920), 320.

20. A. Caldecott, "International and Inter-racial Relations," *The Sociological Review* (1910), 22.

21. George Frederickson, *Black Image in the White Mind, The Debate on Afro-American Character and Destiny 1817–1914* (New York, 1971), 255, 30–34, 327–30; Idus A. Newby, *Jim Crow's Defense: Anti-Negro Thought in America, 1900–1930* (Baton Rouge, 1965).

22. James H. Tufts, "Darwin and Evolutionary Ethics," *The Psychological Bulletin*, XVI (1909), 195–206; Edmund B. Huey, "The Present State of the Binet Scale of Tests for The Measurement of Intelligence," *The Psychological Bulletin*, IX (1912), 160–67; R. S. Woodworth, "Comparative Psychology of Races," *The Psychological Bulletin*, XIII (1916), 388–97 and notes there cited; Franz Boas, *The Mind of Primitive Man* (New York, 1911).

23. Thomas R. Garth, "A Review of Racial Psychology," *Psychological Bulletin*, XXII (1925), 343–64 and notes there cited; Fredrickson, *Black Image in the White Mind*, 327–30; Audrey M. Shuey, *The Testing of Negro Intelligence* (New York, 1966).

24. David W. Southern, *The Malignant Heritage: Yankee Progressives and The Negro Question 1901–1914* (Chicago, 1968); NAACP, *Thirty Years of Lynching in the United States, 1889–1918* (New York, 1919); Arthur Raper, *The Tragedy of Lynching* (Chapel Hill, 1933).

25. Berry, *Black Resistance/White Law*, Chapters 8–12, *passim*.

26. Robert L. Zangrando, "The NAACP and A Federal Anti-Lynching Bill, 1934–40," *Journal of Negro History*, L (April, 1965), 106–17.

27. Richard Dalfiume, "The Forgotten Years of the Negro Revolution," *The Journal of American History*, LV (June, 1968), 90–106.

Notes to RACE & ECONOMY IN THE SOUTH
by Robert Higgs

1. This and the following section draw heavily on economic and demographic data contained in Harvey S. Perloff *et al.*, *Regions, Resources, and Economic Growth* (Baltimore, 1960), and in Simon Kuznets *et al.*, *Population Redistribution and Economic Growth: United States, 1870–1950* (3 vols.; Philadelphia, 1957, 1960, 1964). Related historical details are surveyed by C. Vann Woodward, *Origins of the New South, 1877–1913* ([Baton Rouge], 1951) and by George Brown Tindall, *The Emergence of the New South, 1913–1945* ([Baton Rouge], 1967).

154 Notes

2. U.S. Bureau of the Census, *Historical Statistics of the United States, Colonial Times to 1970* (Washington, 1975), Pt. I, pp. 200, 211, 517–18.

3. Gary S. Becker, *The Economics of Discrimination* (2nd ed.; Chicago, 1971), 140.

4. Robert Higgs, *Competition and Coercion: Blacks in the American Economy, 1865–1914* (New York, 1977), 95–102, 144–46.

5. William Edward Vickery, "The Economics of the Negro Migration, 1900–1960" (Ph.d. dissertation, University of Chicago, 1969), 72, 74, 86. Careful readers will notice that these various estimates are inconsistent. If the relative income of southern blacks was two-thirds in 1900 and did not change substantially during the period 1900–1940, then it could not have been four-tenths in 1940. I recognize that my estimate for 1900 may be in error, but Vickery's estimate of a flat trend may also be wrong, and indeed even the 1940 census data may be wide of the true mark. Reconciliation of these differing estimates would require a difficult but valuable research effort.

6. Vivian W. Henderson, *The Economic Status of Negroes: In the Nation and in the South* (Atlanta, 1963), 15.

7. Becker, *The Economics of Discrimination*, first published in 1957; Donald Dewey, "Negro Employment in Southern Industry," *Journal of Political Economy*, LX (August, 1952), 287–88. See also Gunnar Myrdal, *An American Dilemma: The Negro Problem and Modern Democracy* (New York, 1944), 395.

8. Dewey, "Negro Employment," 283–84.

9. *Ibid.*, 288.

10. Higgs, *Competition and Coercion*, 63–66.

11. Robert Higgs, "Patterns of Farm Rental in the Georgia Cotton Belt, 1880–1900," *Journal of Economic History*, XXXIV (June, 1974), 477–79; Robert Higgs, "Race, Tenure, and Resource Allocation in Southern Agriculture, 1910," *Journal of Economic History*, XXXIII (March, 1973), 151–59; Higgs, *Competition and Coercion*, 66–68.

12. See the sources cited in Higgs, *Competition and Coercion*, 164, n 59; Robert Higgs, "Firm-Specific Evidence on Racial Wage Differentials and Workforce Segregation," *American Economic Review*, LXVII (March, 1977), 236–45.

13. Higgs, "Racial Wage Differentials," 240–43; Myrdal, *American Dilemma*, 1094.

14. Higgs, "Racial Wage Differentials," 239–40, 243–44.

15. *Ibid.*, 241–42.

16. Higgs, *Competition and Coercion*, 90–93; Robert Higgs, "Participation of Blacks and Immigrants in the American Merchant Class, 1890–1910: Some Demographic Relations," *Explorations in Economic History*, XIII (April, 1976), 153–64.

17. Arthur F. Raper, *The Tragedy of Lynching* (Chapel Hill, 1933), 480–81; Tindall, *Emergence of the New South*, 554.

18. Emmett J. Scott, *Negro Migration during the War* (New York, 1920), 72.

19. *Ibid.*, 87–89, 94.

Notes to THE COST OF SEGREGATION
by George B. Tindall

1. Lewis H. Blair, *A Southern Prophecy: The Prosperity of the South Dependent Upon the Elevation of the Negro* (1889), edited with an introduction by C. Vann Woodward (Boston, 1964), quotations that follow from pp. 25–26, 69–70, 88, 95, 148.
2. Philip D. Swenson, "The Not So Strange Career of Jim Crow in Tennessee," *Reviews in American History*, V (June, 1977), 254.
3. Vernon Lane Wharton, *The Negro in Mississippi* (Chapel Hill, 1974); George B. Tindall, *South Carolina Negroes, 1877–1900* (Columbia, S.C., 1952). See also Joel Williamson (ed.), *The Origins of Segregation* (Boston, 1968).
4. David M. Potter, "C. Vann Woodward," in Marcus Cunliffe (ed.), *Postmasters: Some Essays on American Historians* (New York, 1969), 398.
5. Richard Kluger, *Simple Justice: The History of Brown v. Board of Education and Black America's Struggle for Equality* (New York, 1976).
6. C. Vann Woodward, *The Strange Career of Jim Crow* (3rd rev. ed.; New York, 1974).
7. Joel Williamson, *After Slavery: The Negro in South Carolina During Reconstruction, 1861–1877* (Chapel Hill, 1965), 275, 298.
8. C. Vann Woodward, "The Strange Career of a Historical Controversy," in Woodward, *American Counterpoint: Slavery and Racism in the North-South Dialogue* (Boston, 1971), 242.
9. Pierre L. van den Berghe, *Race and Racism: A Comparative Perspective* (New York, 1967); Philip Mason, *Prospero's Magic: Some Thoughts on Class and Race* (London, 1962).
10. Mason, *Prospero's Magic*, 27–33, cited in Woodward, "The Strange Career of a Historical Controversy," 245.
11. Blair, *A Southern Prophecy*, 66.
12. Langston Hughes, *Simple Takes a Wife* (New York, 1953), 85.
13. Carl N. Degler, *Neither Black nor White: Slavery and Race Relations in Brazil and the United States* (New York, 1971).
14. Howard N. Rabinowitz, *Race Relations in the Urban South, 1865–1890* (New York, 1978).
15. Ibid., 001 00.
16. See especially Lawrence W. Levine, *Black Culture and Black Consciousness: Afro-American Folk Thought from Slavery to Freedom* (New York, 1977).
17. George E. Mowry, *Another Look at the Twentieth-Century South* (Baton Rouge, 1973), 81.
18. Stephen J. De Canio, *Agriculture in the Postbellum South: The Economics of Production and Supply* (Cambridge, Mass., 1974); Robert Higgs, *Competition and Coercion: Blacks in the American Economy, 1865–1914* (Cambridge, New York, 1977); Roger L. Ransom and Richard Sutch, *One Kind of Freedom: The Economic Consequence of Emancipation* (Cambridge, London, New York, Melborne, 1977).

19. Harold D. Woodman, "Sequel to Slavery: The New History Views the Postbellum South," *Journal of Southern History*, XLIII (November, 1977), 523–54.

20. Gary S. Becker, *The Economics of Discrimination* (2nd ed.; Chicago, 1971).

21. De Canio, *Agriculture in the Postbellum South*, 13–14, 239.

22. Ransom and Sutch, *One Kind of Freedom*, 177 and *passim*.

23. Higgs, *Competition and Coercion*, 134.

24. Rupert B. Vance, *Human Factors in Cotton Culture* (Chapel Hill, 1929).

25. Rupert B. Vance, "Beyond the Fleshpots: The Coming Culture Crisis in the South," *Virginia Quarterly Review*, XLI (Spring, 1965), 217.

26. Woodman, "Sequel to Slavery," 544–49.

27. George B. Tindall, "Southern Negroes Since Reconstruction: Dissolving the Static Image," in Arthur S. Link and Rembert W. Patrick, *Writing Southern History: Essays in Historiography in Honor of Fletcher M. Green* (Baton Rouge, 1965), 338.

28. *Ibid.*, 361. See also Gunnar Myrdal, "The Negro Problem: A Prognosis," *The New Republic*, CXLVII (July 9, 1962), 11, and Myrdal, *An American Dilemma: The Negro Problem and Modern Democracy* (New York and London, 1944), 997–1024.

DATE DUE

APR 2 9 1983		